PUBLISHED BY:

HAYES PRESS Publisher, Resources & Media,

The Barn, Flaxlands

Royal Wootton Bassett

Swindon, SN4 8DY

United Kingdom

www.hayespress.org

CW01499606

BIBLE VERSIONS:

CHAPTER ONE: HOSEA – ISRAEL'S UNFAITHFULNESS AND GOD'S FAITHFUL LOVE (STEPHEN MCCABE)

"Go, take to yourself a wife of harlotry."[1] It is shocking! Hosea's call as a prophet was one of utter pain and anguish: his first instruction from God was to marry, to love, a harlot who would be unfaithful to him - because, bluntly put, that is how God felt about His relationship with Israel. Think of how painful it is when someone you love wilfully hurts you. The closer a person is to you, the deeper that hurt can be. The more of yourself you give, the more vulnerable to such pain you become - and the betrayal of marriage is perhaps the ultimate example from a human perspective. That is how God felt about Israel's unfaithfulness.

Yes: unfaithfulness in marriage is how God chose to display the seriousness of His own great pain to Hosea - nothing short of that could really have communicated to Hosea God's deep love for Israel and, in turn, how deeply He had been betrayed by their going after Canaanite gods. It shows us, should we ever have questioned it, that divine love is not an impersonal thing - in fact, it is our experience of love amplified infinitely, and thus even more vulnerable than human love in its tireless pursuit of, and commitment to, a people who reject it. God's hurt at having His love spurned is stark in the pages of Hosea.

The kind of vivid imagery used in Hosea resonates with the writings of other prophets explaining God's reasons for exiling Israel: "You adulteress wife, who takes strangers instead of her husband!"[2] The children born to Hosea and Gomer are of note (though the text only explicitly says that the first belonged to Hosea - the others, adding to his hurt, may have been children of harlotry).[3] Their names

The Message of the Minor Prophets

Hayes Press

Published by Hayes Press, 2018.

THE MESSAGE OF THE MINOR PROPHETS

First edition. May 14, 2018.

Copyright © 2018 Hayes Press.

ISBN: 978-1386134411

Written by Hayes Press.

Table of Contents

demonstrate God's displeasure with His people, and are pointers toward the reasons why judgement was coming.[4] The first was Jezreel - because Israel was to be punished for the bloodshed in the town of that name by Jehu[5] and their unchecked attitude to violence and bloodshed. The second was Lo-ruhamah ('she has not obtained compassion'), and the third was Lo-ammi ('not my people'). Each child seems to deepen the gloom and judgment of Israel - for Hosea to name his son 'not my people', instructed by the God of Israel, must have been heart-breaking. For the people of God to be separated from God (in their practices, and then physically, from the Land) was disastrous. Moses had it right centuries earlier when he made the appeal to God, "If your presence does not go with us, do not lead us up from here".[6]

It is a calamitous start, then, to Hosea's message. And yet, despite the bleakness, even by the end of the first chapter, God sends a gracious shaft of light into the situation - a promise of restoration, harking back to the promise given to Abraham[7] (a promise that has not gone away): "Yet the number of the sons of Israel will be like the sand of the sea ... and in the place where it is said to them "You are not My people," it will be said to them, "You are the sons of the living God."[8]

The pattern described above is repeated throughout the book. Judgement is detailed - unavoidable judgement that would surely come (to the Northern Kingdom at the hands of Assyria, to the South by Nebuchadnezzar), which Israel fully deserved for how the people treated God over a sustained period. And yet, after judgement is proclaimed, Hosea consistently and beautifully speaks of the restoration of the faithful who would return to their God (seen in the Southern Kingdom post-Babylon, under the united name of Israel - see Ezra's offering of 12 bulls for all Israel[9]). Thus, again, in the second chapter we see Israel's unfaithfulness condemned by God, but then He speaks of His love: "I will allure her, bring her into the wilderness and speak kindly to her. Then I will give her vineyards from there, and the valley of Achor as a door of hope ... I will say to those who were not My people, "You are My people!" and they will say, "You are my God!"[10]

In this last promise, we see God's purposes overflowing beyond Israel - that in His faithfulness to Israel, He will bless all of the nations such that even those alienated from Him can be brought near, so that we share in the promise.[11] And for Israel in exile, God provides a door of hope in the Valley of Achor (which means 'trouble') - isn't that so characteristic of the faithful love of our God?

Hosea unmistakably shows God to be a God of justice. Chapter 3 emphasises that there will be no 'short cut' through the judgement that Israel faces: "The sons of Israel will remain for many days without king or prince, without sacrifice or sacred pillar and without ephod or household idols. Afterward the sons of Israel will return and seek the LORD their God and David their king ..."[12]

God's Word through Hosea again projects far beyond the return of Israel from exile to a day that still lies in the future for us. A day when Israel will seek YHWH and 'David their king'! What is being prophesied is the resurrection of David to be Prince in restored Israel, which accords with other prophetic writings.[13] The Messiah, great David's greater Son, will rule on earth in the Millennium through delegated authority given to chosen men, with David as Prince over Israel.

It should not escape our attention that the guiltiest people in Israel's unfaithfulness were those who should have known best: the priests, who feed on the sin of My people.[14] How disturbing it is that the people were being led astray by those who should have been set apart for God's service. It is a sober reminder that, of those who have been given much, much will be required.[15]

In Chapter 11, God's faithfulness is openly displayed: "How can I give you up, O Ephraim? How can I surrender you, O Israel? ... My heart is turned over within Me, All My compassions are kindled."[16] God will not give up His people! He will not let them go! Despite the pain that is being caused to Him by their unfaithfulness (demonstrated brutally in Hosea's experience of marriage), He loves them with an everlasting, steadfast, redeeming love[17] - just as Hosea is instructed to love Gomer![18] Not because of their actions (which have been abhorrent to Him) but because of who He is, and because Israel are a part of His purposes - which He will fulfil to His own glory. He cannot deny Himself and His own purposes![19]

The importance of the restoration of Judah for God's purposes is crucial. The majority of the warnings and judgements in Hosea are aimed at the Northern Kingdom of Ephraim/Israel (where Hosea lived). These tribes never recovered after the Assyrian destruction of 722 BC - tragically, they did not listen to the voice of their God (either in warning or through Hosea's prophetic appeal to return). Some people of Ephraim did settle with Judah[20] and respond to Hezekiah's call to reinstitute the Passover.[21] And so, in Judah's restoration (under the corporate name of Israel) we see the hand of God - preparing the scene for the coming of His Son, the Lion of the tribe of Judah.[22] What an expression of His faithfulness!

In the final chapter, Hosea presses home God's appeal to Israel. Return.[23] God did not move; He did not go away from Israel, but they from Him. If they had realised it (if they would yet realise it), God was all they needed: "I will heal their apostasy, I will love them freely ... O Ephraim, what more have I to do with idols? It is I who answer and look after you. I am like a luxuriant cypress; From Me comes your fruit."[24]

One day the restoration will be full, and Israel will be restored to her place as God wills, as Gomer was restored to Hosea.[25] But how wonderful that the same faithful God has expressed His faithfulness to us in His own Son.[26] We may falter in our relationship with God, but we can be so thankful that God's faithfulness is absolute - He cannot deny Himself. The final appeal to Israel is for us as well - God meets our needs. Our fruit comes from Him. It is He who answers and looks after us. Let us depend on His faithfulness.

Bible quotations from the NASB.

CHAPTER TWO: HOSEA – LOVE BEYOND DEGREE (KARL SMITH)

Hosea's meaning is simple, but you can miss it. The Lord Jesus said to the Pharisees, "If you had known what this means, 'I desire mercy, and not sacrifice', you would not have condemned the guiltless."[27] Its original audience understood perfectly what it meant. They were worshipping God. The trouble was, they were worshipping idols as well and committing terrible acts of injustice - just as we sometimes try to combine a Sunday Christianity with other things completely incompatible with following Christ. God was showing them graphically how He felt about it.

We only read about Hosea in his own book, yet we know the most intimate details of his personal life. He had married a woman named Gomer, knowing she would be unfaithful to him, and indeed, after her marriage, she went back to those who had previously paid for her favours.[28] Hosea must have been a public figure. God clearly expected the nation to notice what was happening to him. As with today's celebrities, his private life was public property. Everyone, we can be sure, would have been hungry for the juicy details. He had to deal not only with the hurt of betrayal, but also with the shame of everyone in Israel knowing about it.

Gomer's love for Hosea soon faded, prompting God's question, "What shall I do with you, O Ephraim? What shall I do with you, O Judah? Your love is like a morning cloud, like the dew that goes early away."[29] We've all been fired up after Bible camps, week-ends and special meetings, where we made all sorts of promises - and really meant them. But we're soon back in our ordinary circumstances and the love we wanted to show sometimes seems to fizzle out very quickly. But God doesn't stop loving us. His words, through another prophet, "'I have loved you with an everlasting love"[30], are illustrated in Hosea's continuing love for Gomer. Humiliating as it must have been for him, he bought off the man she had gone to live with and brought her home, promising to look after her[31]. She would never have forgotten this. We need to keep our love for God fresh by reflecting daily on the price he so lovingly paid to buy us back at Calvary.

Hosea must have spent over thirty-five years pleading 'Return, O Israel, to the LORD your God'[32] to have preached within the reigns of all the kings mentioned in the book's first verse. Amazingly, even with the example of his marriage before them, they didn't listen. The Assyrians marched in and took the ten tribes captive at the end of this period and, unlike Judah, they were never returned. Nevertheless, God's forgiving love is unending. Before the first chapter is finished, God interrupts his account of the coming judgement with the promise that one day all twelve tribes of Israel will repent and be saved: "And the children of Judah and the children of Israel shall be gathered together, and they shall appoint for themselves one head."[33] It hasn't happened yet. We, whether Jew or Gentile, who once were not a people, are God's people today[34], but Romans 9-11 reminds us that God will have mercy on his Old Testament people again.

Chapter 11 moves from a husband's love to that of a father. Painstakingly and affectionately, God taught His people "to walk and bent down ... and fed them."[35] It would have broken his heart to punish His metaphorical son: "How can I give you up, O Ephraim? ... My heart recoils within me; my compassion grows warm and tender."[36] Yet He did give up his literal only begotten Son so that He could save us, His sons with a small 's', from deserved judgement and bring us to glory. How His heart must have hurt, but how much He must have loved us. No wonder He desires mercy, not sacrifice: He has made the ultimate sacrifice and the mercy shown here is the meaning of all the Old Testament sacrifices.

We're back to the Lord's quotation from Hosea to the Pharisees, who were observing most of the technicalities of the house of God, bringing their sacrifices and keeping the appointed times correctly, but they had lost sight of the mercy, love and holiness that worship in that place was all about. God wants us to have both. Let's make sure in our day and age that we don't content ourselves with the first only or God will feel much the same as He did in Hosea's time!

Bible quotations from the English Standard Version.

CHAPTER THREE: HOSEA – BOOK OF SALVATION (MARTIN ARCHIBALD)

Why read a book that was already about 800 years old when the Lord was here? A good reason is that it teaches us about the things He values. Further, Paul used it to help Jewish Christians in Rome to understand one of the most difficult truths of the gospel[37]; so it surely should not surprise us if we also find help there.

But perhaps you are still doubtful about learning from a book, like the children who gathered round in the evenings when Jim Elliott and his team were working in Ecuador. One watched the doctor and his assistant updating records, and then said, "Don't you people ever get tired of paper? These two, all they do is look at paper and write on paper. My father says you men smell like paper. He gets mad at me for smelling of paper when I come home from school."

Well, if we smell more like Bibles after prayerfully reading Hosea, it may help our witness at least! The point is that such a book can have a powerful effect on us, its words staying in our minds and shaping our thoughts for our good. 'Hosea' means 'salvation' and we shall find this theme recurring as we unroll the book together.

The Writer's World

First, a little of the writer's world. He dates his book with the reigns of four kings, the first two of which should give us the flavour. Uzziah's reign is the story of success that went wrong. He was a great builder, whose towers made Jerusalem famous again. He brought victory in battle, and equipped the army with new designs for military engineering. The annalist wrote, As long as he sought the LORD, God gave him success.[38] But when he grew powerful, he became proud. He was so sure he knew best that he took on himself to handle sacred things, in defiance of those who had authority in the Temple. It was a fatal mistake: he lost his position and ruined his career. Yet the little we are told about those last wasted years is still instructive. Isaiah himself included them in his records[39]; and Uzziah was given the distinction of being buried with his fathers, in the burial field of the kings. Are we also in danger of resisting the advice of our brothers and sisters in spiritual things, self-satisfied in our own judgement? How much we may also lose! How much we may also withhold in this way from the service of the Lord!

What about the people Uzziah left behind, whom he otherwise would have expected to lead for the years of his ripeness? The young king did what was right before the Lord. Like his father, he was a builder - cities, castles, and towers. Like him he was victorious in war. So Jotham became mighty, because he ordered his ways before the LORD his God.[40] Yet the people continued their corrupt practices;[41] as though, when Uzziah failed, the people lost direction and did not recover till long after.

What's in a Name?

The Book of salvation begins with names for new babies. When the first son was born, the Lord said, "Call him Jezreel, because I will soon punish the house of Jehu for the massacre at Jezreel, and I will put an end to the kingdom of Israel."[42] What had Jehu done to deserve this judgement? Jezreel was the home of Ahab and Jezebel, and Jehu avenged on their house the blood of Naboth, and their promotion of the worship of Baal, but went far beyond his brief in the numbers he slew. Further, he did break the alliance of Judah's kings with the family of Ahab, but let the people continue to use the altars in Israel. Because the king did not make connection with the place of the Lord's Name in Jerusalem, the people still could not see past the worship of Baal, the male fertility god. They needed to return to the Lord Jehovah, the God of the whole family. He was the God of Abraham who could give him a son of his own even in his old age; the God who could give Paul a great spiritual family, though he was unmarried for the kingdom's sake.[43]

So it may be that we also need to appreciate that the same God has His purpose in whatever hinders us from marriage or family, for God sets the lonely in families. He leads forth the prisoners with singing, if we will accept His own wonderful way and time.[44]

The Lord's Own Sowing

Looking a little deeper now in Hosea 1, we find that 'Jezreel' means 'God sows'. This was the God of the lone pilgrim, like Abraham, of whom he made a great family. By autumn, and in any case, in the Western world the farmer has assessed his last crop, and decided what to sow for the coming season. Some may have already sown the winter crop. Some may be disheartened, or just have delayed, doing nothing to the purpose.

A sluggard does not plough in season; so at harvest time he looks but finds nothing.[45] Yes, living for God often means hard work at a difficult time. The Lord also spoke on this: The sower went forth to sow ... You remember He was speaking about types of ground and their fruitfulness. The Sower may now be asking us, How is your soil? What has the crop been like in the last five years - a hundred-fold, thirty-fold, or choked with weeds? In Luke 8:14 (RV) the thorns are interpreted as cares and riches and pleasures of this life. The Lord did not need to explain any further.

Yet Hosea's final message on this is "... great will be the day of Jezreel"[46] when God in his mercy will sow the field again, a promise for Israel's national future. May He be as merciful with us, before life's opportunity passes by for ever, for the next name carries a chilling warning.

No More Mercy?

The second child was to be called Lo-Ruhamah[47]: no more mercy, no pardon of any sort. How thankful believers in Christ should be that our salvation is secure for eternity! It was not achieved by our efforts, and so cannot be interfered with by any thought or action of ours. But the point may come when the Lord has spoken to us often enough about a besetting sin, or wrong attitude without response, and there can be mercy no longer to rescue some area (or all!) of our life's service for Him. We ask gently if some reader has a weight problem that hinders you in the race of Hebrews 12:1: some besetting sin, or burdensome grudge. Why carry such baggage all the road, always getting in the way of more fruitful service we could give? Then at the close, see so much burned up in the judgement day? Someone has written: *"If I think of the world, I get the impress of the world; if I think of my trials and sorrows, I get the impress of my trials and sorrows; if I think of my failures, I get the impress of my failures; if I think of Christ, I get the impress of Christ".*

With a People or By Myself?

The third child's name would seem to Israel or Judah to add insult to injury. The Lord said, "Call him Lo-Ammi, for you are not my people, and I am not your God."[48] It would take great courage for the prophet to explain this name to people who prided themselves on being special to God. Yet we have no doubt that God still longed that Israel would accept the terms on which they could claim to be His people in truth. Today as He looks on the nations in their self-assertive, grasping pride, how much He still desires to have a people who distinctively belong to Him, and so show His character, and the order of His rule in this world! Therefore the enemy is making a determined effort to sap the resolve of believers in Churches of God to express this ideal together, and to claim its many blessings.

To test how successful the enemy has been, we may compare our record with that of the first Church of God, in Jerusalem, in the early chapters of Acts. In those great days, they were one in heart and mind in material care for one another.[49] When they prayed, they raised their voices with one accord.[50] Today, however, how many are together at the time announced on the Church of God noticeboard for the assembly prayers? Do we still need to be shown that a church that is short of 100 per cent involvement in prayer together is by that much weaker in all its functions? Oh, you say, but we have nearly all the roll present for the Breaking of Bread! Then let us ask ourselves, how many are active in the flow of thanksgiving - from the opening of the meeting, coming with an offering ready to give? Is there a variety of voices and willing hands for the first service of the emblems upon our Lord's table? Sisters, are you also exercised to come for your silent offering with hearts full and overflowing?

What can we do, so that we may all be recognized as sons of the living God?[51] We each need to examine ourselves before we dare to join in the communion we are called to week by week. God bless those who meet as prayer-partners and groups; may they help to bridge the gaps that divide young from old, and 'core' from 'fringe', so that all are together in the assembly 'powerhouse'. Then, brothers, let us help others to listen to the end when we rise to lead the assembly in thanksgiving or prayer,

- with a voice that all can hear;

- with fresh words that all can appreciate;

- with thought for the concerns of all;

- with a clear progression through a recognizable theme.

And when Bible conference time comes round, can we help each other to be together, saying by our actions, "I love the word of God; I belong with His churches; and I want to encourage others with my presence before Him." "Say of your brothers, 'My people', and of your sisters, 'My loved one'".[52]

Sometimes we realize how much we forget that God gives us all that we have, and we do not take time to thank Him, or to praise Him to others. Then we wonder why we don't seem to get opportunities for witness, and why people become embarrassed when we do speak up for our Saviour. Asaph recovered a proper perspective, when he was upset about another matter, by returning to the light of the sanctuary. When he had worked through his problem there, he acknowledged, But as for me, it is good to be near God. I have made the Sovereign LORD my refuge; I will tell of all your deeds.[53]

Do we have much more to say about food and drink, like those whose hope is in this life alone? Perhaps our friends recognize us as those who lead the discussion of fashion. Meanwhile the Eternal Lover of our souls, who has clothed us with the garments of salvation, has to wait for a mention before bed, or a quick thanks at meals (if no-one's watching), or just a minute in the morning - no more!

Then we need not be surprised if we begin to find thorns and weeds instead of fruitfulness, when we look over the year's spiritual programme in the assembly business meeting. Did not the Lord warn us about this, when He asked us (how many times?) about our own ground condition? But we preferred to put the effort into those cares and riches and pleasures of this life.[54] May we take heed, before the Lord has to block our path with the pain of thorn bushes and wall us in.

"What More Have I to Do With Idols?"

"Return, O Israel, to the LORD your God ... Take words with you and return to the LORD."[55]

So the prophet calls us to personal repentance; and then to communion, as we "offer the fruit of our lips." If we confess our sins, He is faithful and righteous to forgive us our sins, and to cleanse us from all unrighteousness. The Lover who poured out His feelings in the Song of Songs appealed: "... show me your face, let me hear your voice; for your voice is sweet, and your face is lovely."[56]

Is it right, is it natural to neglect to take time in His presence, in communion with our Lord, who redeemed us at such cost? First, of course, we must remember that He redeemed us from an empty way of life.[57] We may need to make more progress in the way He set us on, with a new song in our mouths, else we will find that we have nothing to speak about to Him. Let us return, and take words we have prepared, fit for Him to hear.

But there is another dimension to enter into, because the appeal from Hosea's last chapter is couched in the plural: the Lord was addressing a people. The Lover of the Song called, "You who dwell in the gardens with friends in attendance, let me hear your voice".[58] Once in the first garden, the voice of God was heard as He walked in the cool of the day, and the man and the woman came gladly to listen and reply. He who restores our souls longs to renew that exchange, to hear our voice! And when we "offer the fruit of lips" together, there is nothing to equal the communion that Christ offers at His altar when

His people come to worship, to speak and to sing of their great God and Saviour. The garden of the Song is a garden enclosed, shut up for God's own possession, and it is a people that fully express the joys of which it speaks; God's "tilled land" of 1 Corinthians 3:9 (RV margin). Let us return there with full hearts, that our High Priest may also have something to offer. For, "What have we to do with idols. Who have companied with Him?"

CHAPTER FOUR: JOEL – THE PROPHET OF THE DAY OF THE LORD (STEPHEN HICKLING)

Very little is known about Joel or the circumstances surrounding his prophecy. The central theme of Joel's prophecy, though, is hard to miss; there are five references in this short book to the day of the Lord.[59] Given the problems with supplying the historical context to his message, it is difficult to comment definitively on whether Joel bore witness to events which had already befallen the land of Judah in his day or spoke only of things in his (and the nation's) future; it is, perhaps, no less difficult to determine whether to interpret his language literally or allegorically.

It seems, though, that we can discern that in speaking of the day of the Lord, Joel's words were intended to have both a partial near and ultimate far fulfilment. In other words, Joel appears to have regarded the day of the Lord as an event occurring in instalments, with interludes between the instalments. The devastating combination of locust plague and drought, whether we regard it as having occurred or still future at the time of Joel's prophecy, was intended to be a warning sign to Judah of a fast-approaching day of judgment. The day of the Lord was 'near' for Judah in Joel's day.[60] We can only speculate as to the historical fulfilment of the judgment which Joel foretold - the Assyrian invasion or the Babylonian exile of Judah, perhaps.

Yet, Joel also seems to have anticipated the future, climactic fulfilment of the day of the Lord. His change of focus is evident from verse 28 of chapter 2 onwards; from there he turns to deal with events which would take place in those days and at that time.[61] He forecasts the repentance of the nation and their return to God who, abounding in lovingkindness, receives and restores them. And it is after this,[62] - that is, after the repentance and restoration of Judah - that Joel foresees this consummation of the day of the Lord unfolding.

The Timing of the Eschatological Day of the Lord

We believe that the day of the Lord, which Joel viewed from afar, still remains in the future; it is clearly much nearer to us than it was to the prophet, though. Helpfully, Joel gives us some important indicators regarding the timing of this future instalment. He tells us that:

- there will be tremendous celestial disturbances before the day of the Lord, namely that the sun will be turned to darkness and the moon to blood and that the stars will lose their brightness;[63] and

- multitudes of people will be gathered to the valley of decision before the day of the Lord.[64]

This information is supplemented by other Old and New Testament references to the day of the Lord, which tell us that:

- God will send 'Elijah the prophet' before the day of the Lord;[65]

- the apostasy, which is thought to mean the great rebellion of earth's inhabitants against their creator, must come before the day of the Lord;[66] and

- the man of lawlessness, the son of destruction (elsewhere described as the antichrist[67] and as the beast[68]) will be revealed and will take his seat in the temple of God in Jerusalem before the day of the Lord.[69]

There is clear synergy between what Joel said about the celestial disturbances, which would precede the day of the Lord, and the Lord's own words about the same in His discourse on the Mount of Olives. Indeed, it is quite possible that the Lord was mindful of Joel's words and exposited them in His own teaching, when He said: "But immediately after the tribulation of those days THE SUN WILL BE DARKENED, AND THE MOON WILL NOT GIVE ITS LIGHT, AND THE STARS WILL FALL from the sky, and the powers of the heavens will be shaken. And then the sign of the Son of Man will appear in the sky, and then all the tribes of the earth will mourn, and they will see the SON OF MAN COMING ON THE CLOUDS OF THE SKY with power and great glory." [70]

The Lord taught that these celestial events will occur at the end of Daniel's 70th week, immediately after the great tribulation[71] and just before the return of the Son of Man. Taking the Lord's teaching together with Joel's, we can then establish that this future instalment[72] of the day of the Lord comes at the end of the tribulation period and that it commences with the coming of the King of Kings and Lord of Lords to judge the nations of the world.[73]

The Nature of the Day of the Lord

Joel leaves us in no doubt about the nature of the day of the Lord; it will come as destruction from the Almighty.[74] It is a day without equal in its darkness and gloom. It is a great and terrible day, in which human strength will be shattered. Throughout Scripture, the day of the Lord is primarily linked with the theme of God's judgment of the nations at the time of the Lord's return to the earth. Joel records that it will be a day of judgment for all the nations, though he mentions certain nations, which are seen to be especially deserving of wrath (Tyre, Sidon, Philistia, Egypt and Edom) on account of their hatred for, and violence towards, Israel.

What Significance for Us?

Since we have seen that the day of the Lord commences with Christ's second coming to the earth we might, perhaps, wonder what relevance Joel's message has to the Christian who, we believe, will have been raptured before then. The apostle Paul taught quite clearly that the day of the Lord will not be a day of loss for the Christian.[75] Praise God that, by His grace, we are sons of light and sons of day!

Nonetheless, Paul (just like Joel and other Old Testament prophets) considered it necessary to instruct God's people concerning the day of the Lord. Why? We can discern at least three reasons, which underpin both Joel and Paul's ministry:

• The day of the Lord teaches us about the character of our God and, in so doing, is an encouragement to us.[76] It reminds us that there is a righteous Judge and that, in His time, He will bring the nations to account, vindicating His people such that they will never again be put to shame.[77] As those who have called on the name of the Lord, we are not destined for God's wrath, which will be poured out on opposing nations on the day of the Lord; rather God has chosen us to obtain salvation through our Lord Jesus Christ.[78] It is important that we grasp this in order that, notwithstanding the increase of lawlessness that we see all around, our love does not grow cold and our composure may not be easily shaken.[79]

• The day of the Lord is instructive to us in our conduct as disciples of the Lord Jesus. Joel's message was for all the inhabitants of the land: from the priest to the farmer, even to the drunkard. And the message was simple: wake up;[80] sorrow for sin;[81] and repent.[82]Paul, too, tells us that an understanding of the day of the Lord compels alertness and sobriety.[83] Our election to salvation should not operate as a licence for sin; rather we should walk worthily of those who are of the day since, by His grace, we know that we are to live together with Him.

• The day of the Lord informs our witness. We understand that the day of the Lord will take this world by surprise; at a time when the nations are declaring peace, they will be overtaken by inescapable destruction. The day will come upon them like a thief in the night; a day of great loss.[84]Doesn't our understanding give us a sense of urgency in our witness? Joel knew that his message must reach all the inhabitants of the land. We will also want to tell our 'sons' about it, and our neighbours and colleagues too. Won't we, like Joel, raise the alarm[85]for the day of the Lord is coming; surely it is near!

Bible references from the NASB, unless stated otherwise.

CHAPTER FIVE: JOEL – WHY DOES GOD ALLOW IT? (MARTIN JONES)

Joel had it tough. Not only did he have to suffer a locust plague eating the people out of house and home, he then had to inform his neighbours that their suffering was entirely their own fault. Even worse, the suffering was deliberately and directly inflicted by their God - the graphic army of locusts being described as the Lord's! Though unlikely to win any popularity contests, at least Joel could console himself that he had an answer which has eluded many suffering people today who ask, "Why?!"

This isn't some dry philosophical debating point, but a cry borne of bewilderment, frustration and pain. "Why me? Why not someone else? It's not fair! Why didn't God stop this? What have I done to deserve this? I thought He cared!" Instinctively, we assume that suffering is 'deserved' as part of a relatively simple 'cause and effect' model (e.g. Sodom and Gomorrah).

But when a tower collapsed in Jerusalem, killing eighteen people, Jesus warned against prematurely concluding that this tragic event was a summary judgement by God on people who were more wicked than anyone else.[86] Plainly, God was not involved in that calamity in the same way as he had been in Joel's locust plague. He permitted it but He did not prescribe it.

Similarly, the Pharisees assumed a man born blind was "'steeped in sin from birth'" and asked who was to blame. Jesus told them the real point was that the affliction afforded an opportunity to bring glory to God by its removal.[87] In answering, "Why?" it may be helpful to consider three sources of suffering: 1) humanity, 2) 'nature' and 3) God Himself. We have to concede that much of the suffering in the world is caused by what has been called 'man's inhumanity to man'. God has given us the gift of free will to act as we please, but operating within a universe of cause and effect. The physical, moral and social consequences of what we do are therefore inescapable, and so our responsibility is equally inescapable. How easy would it be for God to stop each wrong decision or act, and the next one ... and the next one ...? But very quickly there would be no free will at all. And so God has graciously honoured that gift of free will by allowing its natural, and often terrible, consequences to occur even to today.

The constant stream of natural disasters that occur can also be traced back to a consequence of free will - the disobedience of Adam.[88] In some sense, the cursing of the ground reflects the dislocation in the relationship between Creator and created, whether human or not. Until the relationship is restored, the created will continue to malfunction - a situation first to be addressed in the millennial reign of Christ, but comprehensively only when there is a new heaven and a new earth. Until then, none are guaranteed immunity from so-called 'acts of God', irrespective of their moral condition or spiritual status. We can be sure it's always safe to treat calamitous events as 'a wake-up call' in realizing how small, frail and exposed we are, and how much we need to rely on God for our very breath and, vitally, our spiritual future.

Thirdly, as in Joel's experience, suffering can be caused by God's judgement, against believers or unbelievers. The end purpose of each, whilst we are still in the age of grace, is to turn us back to Him. This type of suffering can therefore be a catalyst for vital change in our lives - although it doesn't seem pleasant, helpful or even warranted at the time.

It's facile to suggest such a complex question can ever be completely answered! But it has helpfully been said that a fabric viewed through a magnifying glass is clear in the middle and blurred at the edges. We only know the edges are clear because of what we see in the middle. Life's fabric has many blurred edges - events and circumstances we do not understand - but they must be interpreted by the clarity we see in the centre: the cross of Christ. We aren't left to guess about the goodness and intentions of God from isolated bits of data. God has clearly revealed His character and dramatically demonstrated it to us in the Cross. "He who did not spare His own Son, but delivered Him up for us all, how shall He not with Him also freely give us all things?"[89]

CHAPTER SIX: AMOS – SCOURGE OF THE COMPLACENT (KARL SMITH)

Amos was not a career prophet. He was a humble man from a humble background: "I was no prophet, nor a prophet's son, but I was a herdsman and a dresser of sycamore figs. But the LORD took me from following the flock, and the LORD said to me, 'Go, prophesy to my people Israel.'" [90] Then, as now, neither intellect nor family tradition qualify the man of God, but only the call of the Lord to the work.

Israel was split into two kingdoms, Israel and Judah, when Amos preached. He grew up in Judah, among the shepherds of Tekoa in the days of Uzziah king of Judah and in the days of Jeroboam the son of Joash, king of Israel.[91] Uzziah was a good king and had brought military security and prosperity to Jerusalem. Later in life, however, he wanted to do everything himself and died for trying, against the will of God, to be not only king, but priest as well. Jeroboam II, by contrast, was as bad as the previous king of that name, who had split the kingdom in the first place and made the northern kingdom descend into idolatry.[92] Nevertheless, this was a settled time in the history of both Israelite states and a lot of people were able to take life easy. Amos would have preached at the same time as Jonah north of the border[93] and just before Isaiah's main writings.[94]

Thank goodness we're not like them! Many of Amos's first listeners would have been comfortable enough with the first chapter. It denounced their enemies one after another. It started with the Syrians, who were the main threat to their security. Punishment was coming upon them because they have threshed Gilead with threshing sledges of iron.[95] The picture is a graphic one. These sledges were pulled by oxen over the grain after the harvest to beat it out so that the grain could be separated from the useless chaff. It means they had crushed this area of Israel on the far side of the Jordan. It was one of the first areas to go when the LORD began to cut off parts of Israel.[96] At the beginning of Jeroboam II's reign, the LORD saw that the affliction of Israel was very bitter[97] because of the Syrians. The message therefore that, "I will break the gate-bar of Damascus" [98] would have been a popular opening. Indeed the Lord in His amazing mercy and compassion gave Jeroboam strength to recapture lost territory and even the Syrian cities of Damascus and Hamath themselves.[99] Amos's prophecy that "the people of Syria shall go into exile to Kir" was fulfilled about three decades later when their northern neighbours Assyria overtook them in power.[100]

Having despatched the Syrians, Amos deals with the other neighbours. The reasons for their downfall is clear. Each section begins, "For three transgressions ... and for four, I will not revoke the punishment." [101] But just as our imaginary listener is settling down to enjoy himself, Amos brings it closer to home. Thus says the LORD: "For three transgressions of Judah, and for four, I will not revoke the punishment, because they have rejected the law of the LORD, and have not kept his statutes, but their lies have led them astray, those after which their fathers walked. So I will send a fire upon Judah, and it shall devour the strongholds of Jerusalem." [102]

The people were still turning away from God's commandments, their idolatry on Israel's high places still only just under the surface. They had as many sins to confront as the nations around them. Sadly, when generations continued to ignore God, this prophecy was fulfilled as the Babylonians burned Jerusalem with fire.[103]

Israel, too, was going to have to face up to their transgressions. Amos focuses on their oppression of the poor: they sell the righteous for silver, and the needy for a pair of sandals - those who trample the head of the poor into the dust of the earth and turn aside the way of the afflicted.[104] Explicitly ignoring the commandments of the law,[105] they deprived their debtors even of the only clothes they had for warmth. What does God think of today's loan sharks and the more professional failure to show mercy on the part of more reputable financial institutions?

The denunciation of both Israelite kingdoms continues into chapter 4. Then Amos reminds them of the various attempts the Lord had made to discipline them. He intended to get their attention by the disasters brought upon their land. The recurring chorus to the song, however, is "yet you did not return to me."[106] Is the Lord trying to get us to take notice that we are going the wrong way by what He brings into our lives? The New Testament, explaining the Old, reminds us that the Lord disciplines the one he loves and commands: "do not regard lightly the discipline of the Lord".[107] Amos brings out the Lord's sorrow when we stubbornly will not return to Him, the outcome for which He longs.

Amos then takes a long view of Israel's idolatry, going back to their earliest days of travel through the wilderness to the promised land. Stephen quotes Amos 5:25-27 to make this very point to the religious authorities in Jerusalem.[108] What really bothers him is the hypocrisy of trying to combine service in God's house with lack of concern for the poor. Some even professed to look forward to the manifestation of God's glory at the end of time: "Woe to you who desire the day of the LORD! Why would you have the day of the LORD? It is darkness, and not light."[109]

It is easy to say we are a people who desire the Lord's return and reign, but do we share God's rejection of the things for which His wrath is coming, or do we tolerate them in our own lives? Christ has saved us from that coming anger, but it was costly for Him and demands our repentance.

The keynote of the book is the beginning of chapter six: "Woe to those who are at ease in Zion, and to those who feel secure on the mountain of Samaria." Like the New Testament church of God in Laodicea,[110] they presumed on the fact that they were in the right place. "I'm baptised and in the church now, so I can coast for a bit," we can imagine the Laodiceans saying, and all the while the Lord Jesus was outside, knocking at the door. May we never lose our sensitivity to the challenge of the Lord.

One area picked out for special criticism was Bethel. It had been the place of God's revelation to Jacob that He wanted to live in a house on earth.[111] Although Jerusalem was chosen as the place for that house to be built,[112] Bethel was still used by many as a place of pagan worship and in particular, one of the two golden calves that Jeroboam I had originally erected was there.[113] A Jew from the southern kingdom, Amos was not afraid to travel north to denounce what was going on at Bethel.[114] The end of chapter 7 narrates the opposition Amos faced from the priest of the local religion there for his trouble. Those outwardly faithful to the Lord in Judah were not much better, however. They couldn't wait for the service to be over to start making money again![115]

The book ends with an apocalyptic vision of judgement, yet this culminates in a burst of joyful anticipation of the Millennial glory to follow. It emphasizes the people from all nations celebrating the coming Messiah: "'In that day I will raise up the booth of David that is fallen and repair its breaches, and raise up its ruins and rebuild it as in the days of old, that they may possess the remnant of Edom and all the nations who are called by my name,' declares the LORD who does this."[116]

At the very first conference of overseers, James quoted this to demonstrate the Lord's intention to have a people made of both Jews and Gentiles (non-Jews).[117] The whole world will rejoice that Israel is settled in their land. For all the judgement prophesied, repentance and the return of Messiah, who pays for all our sins, will result in wonderful outbursts of joy: "'I will plant them on their land, and they shall never again be uprooted out of the land that I have given them,' says the LORD your God."[118]

Bible quotations from the ESV.

CHAPTER SEVEN: AMOS – MAN'S INHUMANITY TO MAN (CRAIG JONES)

Mankind's seemingly inexhaustible capacity to inflict hardship, suffering, injustice and death upon fellow men, women and children is staggering in its scope. Historians have estimated that up to 170 million people have died at the hands of their own brutal, repressive governments during the 20th century, with the worst culprits being China's Mao Tse-Tung (up to 50 million) and Russia's Joseph Stalin (over 20 million). Quite apart from the consequences of internal or external conflict amongst nations, the inhumane treatment of men, women and children can be seen in many other areas, where the deliberate inaction of governments, organisations, businesses and individuals leads to poverty, famine and disease - whilst those who possess more of the world's material benefits look on in apparent indifference. Such indifference is chillingly summed up by Joseph Stalin: "A single death is a tragedy; a million deaths is a statistic."

It may seem to us that such inhumanity is indeed a 20th century phenomenon - or at least that the 20th century has produced ever more sophisticated and subtle ways in which to inflict it. However, some 750 years before the birth of Christ, God raised up a humble shepherd, Amos, commissioning him as a prophet of God, with an uncompromising message, warning of judgement upon nations who had committed atrocities comparable in their brutality to those we identify in our own recent history (ethnic cleansing, rape, murder, genocide – see chapter 1). This message was also to be taken to those whom God had chosen as His own people, to whom He had promised special privileges and blessings and of whom He expected justice and righteousness to be characteristic of their individual and national consciousness, guiding their actions and policies, setting them apart as an example to the nations round about.

God's chosen people - both the northern kingdom of Israel and the southern kingdom of Judah - had sinned grievously against the Lord, in particular in regard to their mistreatment of the poor and less fortunate.[119] The nation at this time was very prosperous and it seems evident that this prosperity was only enjoyed by the rich, whilst the poor suffered. The rich became richer and consequently more self-indulgent and decadent in their pleasures – well-appointed houses[120], easy living at the expense of others.[121] All this was an affront to God, who, in entering into covenant relationship with His chosen people, made careful and specific provisions for the poor of the community.[122] On top of all this, they had rejected the law of the Lord and had not kept His statutes; their observance of feasts and offerings of sacrifices were empty gestures, devoid of meaning in their own hearts and consequently despised by the Lord Himself.[123] The people had consistently ignored the warnings of impending judgement and now the time had finally come when the Lord had no other option but to bring them into captivity.

As God's people today, there remains for us an expectation from the Lord that a sense of social justice and compassion should characterize our community. In his letter, James warns against an attitude of snobbery and class distinction[124] and also cries out against all those who abuse their wealth and status at the expense of others.[125] Whilst we naturally recoil from the more brutal examples of man's inhumanity to man, and decry the wickedness that motivates such violence, it is nevertheless possible that the underlying attitudes that often reside in the hearts of those responsible for such atrocities may be in evidence in us, albeit subtly; a certain sense of superiority, of partiality towards some people as opposed to others, of not wanting to associate with those who aren't in our 'class', of vanity and the desire for recognition and attention. We do well, therefore, to remember Paul's words to the believers in the church of God in Corinth, "For consider your calling, brethren, that there were not many ... noble; but God has chosen the ... weak things of the world ... and the base things of the world and the despised God has chosen."[126]

As with God's people of old, we have a high and privileged calling and the Lord expects that those who are His chosen ones, above all others, should outwardly reflect His own nature of love, kindness and compassion in their dealings with each other, and with their fellow men, women and children. We are to prove the genuineness of our discipleship by our love and to manifest "the sweet aroma of the knowledge of Him in every place. For we are a fragrance of Christ."[127]

CHAPTER EIGHT: OBADIAH – WHEN OUR STRENGTHS ARE OUR WEAKNESSES (PETER HICKLING)

It is true of nearly everyone that his strengths are directly related to his weaknesses; think on the one hand of the speaker who will always give a superb address, but needs three months notice for it, and on the other of the man who will speak at half an hour's notice, but always does things at the last minute! Closer to home, think of yourself; you can probably put your finger on something - I can! Self-confident people are frequently admired, because they are often successful and free of the miserable feelings of inferiority that plague those who feel that they are failures. Yet the fact that it is self-confidence carries the seeds of disaster. When self-esteem becomes excessive it becomes pride, and pride is at the root of sin - it says 'me first'.

This is portrayed in the book of Obadiah, the shortest book in the Old Testament. It relates to the nation of Edom, which was descended from Jacob's brother Esau, a man full of self-confidence, but who valued the material more than the spiritual - the epitome of the 'fleshly', rather than the spiritual attitude. Edom lived in the mountainous territory to the south of Israel, and they were confident that no-one could dislodge them. One of their strongholds was the rocky defile of Sela, later built up by the Nabateans as Petra, Burgon's rose-red city - 'half as old as time.'[128] However, God warned them that their self-sufficiency was self-deceit: "The pride of your heart has deceived you, you who live in the clefts of the rock, in your lofty dwelling, who say in your heart, "Who will bring me down to the ground?" Though you soar aloft like the eagle, though your nest is set among the stars, from there I will bring you down, declares the LORD."[129]

Similarly, the Edomites were proud of their intellect; their security enabled them to delight in clever sayings and to flaunt their wisdom. Yet God was to bring this down too: "Will I not on that day, declares the LORD, destroy the wise men out of Edom, and understanding out of Mount Esau?"[130]

Don't Edom's attitudes seem familiar in later history? At the height of the British Empire Kipling, seeing the danger, wrote:

For heathen heart that puts her trust

In reeking tube and iron shard -

All valiant dust that builds on dust,

And guarding, calls not Thee to guard -

For frantic boast and foolish word,

Thy mercy on Thy people, Lord![131]

The message to Edom reaches out to us all. Are we so proud of what we have and what men can do that we feel completely self-sufficient? This is self-delusion, as complete as Edom's, for our most fundamental needs cannot be met by possessions and knowledge. Things can be taken away suddenly, as we have seen in the relatively recent Twin Towers attack and the tsunami, and, for example, nuclear physics can bring Chernobyl, as well as cheaper energy. Human character is no better than it ever was; it will only be improved if God changes it, and He will do this by His own means. He says, "'I will destroy the wisdom of the wise, and the discernment of the discerning I will thwart.' ... For since, in the wisdom of God, the world did not know God through wisdom, it pleased God through the folly of what we preach to save those who believe. ... we preach Christ crucified ... the power of God and the wisdom of God."[132]

This was 'folly' by men's standard, of course. In fact, the death of the Christ instead of us was the only way in which we could be brought back to God. There's no room for pride here; the Christian believer has to admit that Christ did for him what he could not do for himself. As a consequence, the words 'proud' and 'Christian' are incompatible. Having said this, of course, it is perfectly proper to take 'pride' - i.e. to find satisfaction - say in a job well done.

The conclusion of all this is that self-confidence is misplaced confidence; boasting about our wealth or intelligence is not only vulgar, but it also betrays a lack of real confidence in God. "Pride goes before destruction, and a haughty spirit before a fall."[133]

Bible quotations are from the English Standard Version.

CHAPTER NINE: JONAH - GOD'S COMPASSION AND JONAH'S LACK OF IT (JOHNNY ARCHIBALD)

Jonah was a prophet, but he was also rebellious. He was told by God to go and preach to an infamous Gentile city far from Israel ... and he refused! The sensational account of 'Jonah and the whale' is familiar to many from Sunday School days and whilst a basic summary of its events has a natural fascination for children, there is a far greater message of God's compassion upon all nations who repent.

Jonah was living in a time of difficulty for Israel; of split kingdoms and the threat of neighbouring enemies, but Jonah was involved in blessing for the people when Jeroboam "... restored the territory of Israel ... according to the word of the LORD God of Israel, which he had spoken through his servant Jonah ... For the LORD saw that the affliction of Israel was very bitter; and whether bond or free, there was no helper for Israel" [134]. Whilst the record in 2 Kings shows the local blessing of the word of the Lord through Jonah, the Book of Jonah begins with the very clear instruction for a mission far from home: "the word of the LORD came to Jonah ... saying, 'Arise, go to Nineveh, that great city, and cry out against it; for their wickedness has come up before Me'" [135].

Nineveh was perhaps not attractive to Jonah for a number of reasons. It had been founded by Nimrod who, in addition to being a 'mighty hunter', was also a prolific builder of cities[136]. Nimrod had come from the line of Ham, son of Noah, who had received a curse, rather than a blessing from Noah. The Philistines had also come from that line, another enemy of God's people, as had the Canaanites generally. Israel, by contrast, came from the line of Shem, the son for whom

Noah sought blessing. In addition to Nineveh's ancient and perhaps despised origin, there was also the very practical matter of its being several hundred miles north-east across arid and hostile country from Jonah's place of birth in Galilee[137].

At the outset of Jonah's assignment the Lord said to Jonah that the city was guilty of wickedness, which would only reinforce the negative aspects of the duty in Jonah's mind. Nineveh was a great city in its size and fame[138], (perhaps taking three days to walk round)[139] and possibly inhabited by families who had a combined 120,000 children, and space for 'much livestock'[140].

A reading of the short book of Nahum (and Zephaniah 2:13-15) provides a great deal more detail on the condition and attitude of the inhabitants of Nineveh a few generations after Jonah's witness in the city. These give a very graphic account of the extent of Nineveh's poor spiritual condition in the sight of the Lord. The site of ancient Nineveh is near the Tigris River and close to modern day Mosul in Iraq. It is instructive to us that even though the Lord knew that, within a few generations of Jonah's preaching, the city would have to be judged severely and destroyed, He still had compassion on the generation living in Jonah's day. This aspect of God's character is highlighted for us in the New Testament when Peter says, "In truth I perceive that God shows no partiality. But in every nation whoever fears Him and works righteousness is accepted by Him"[141].

Jonah was well aware of the compassionate heart of the Lord; when Jonah heard that he was to go and preach to this Gentile city he knew that if they repented then the Lord would relent from doing harm. Jonah claimed that it was for this very reason that he decided that he would try to avoid going to Nineveh by travelling in the very opposite direction, first on land and then by sea. Jonah was so opposed to the idea of the Ninevites escaping from judgment that when they repented at his preaching it displeased Jonah exceedingly, and he became angry[142]. Jonah felt so strongly about the Lord being merciful that he felt that it would be better if the Lord should take his life, "for it is better for me to die than to live!"[143].

Despite Jonah's tantrum, the Lord gave him the opportunity to change his mind by patiently asking him the question; Is it right for you to be angry?[144] Jonah then went out of Nineveh, with the apparent hope that its people may yet commit further wrongdoing and come into judgment. Jonah made a shelter close to the city, so that if the Lord would still judge them, then he would have a prime position to view the destruction.

The Lord provided a plant to give further shade for Jonah from the oppressive sunlight, but when the plant died Jonah had greater pity for the fleeting life of the plant than the potentially severe judgement of the people of Nineveh, with its very substantial infant population and dependent livestock. Jonah is a special book in showing us the compassion of the Lord on Gentiles in the Old Testament. Similarly, in Jeremiah 12 we read of a fascinating conversation between Jeremiah and the Lord. Jeremiah asks why wicked Gentile nations prosper and the Lord answers: "Thus says the LORD: "Against all My evil neighbours who touch the inheritance which I have caused my people Israel to inherit - behold, I will pluck them out of their land and pluck out the house of Judah from among them. Then it shall be, after I have plucked them out, that I will return and have compassion on them and bring them back, everyone to his heritage and everyone to his land. And it shall be, if they will learn carefully the ways of my people, to swear by My name, 'As the LORD lives,' as they taught my people to swear by Baal, then they shall be established in the midst of My people"[145].

The warmth of the compassion of God is also seen touchingly in Lamentations: "For the lord will not cast off for ever. Though He causes grief, yet He will show compassion according to the multitude of His mercies. For He does not afflict willingly, nor grieve the children of men"[146]. We could reasonably expect the approach of God in the Old Testament to be matched in the life of the Lord Jesus Christ, who is "... the fullness of the Godhead bodily"[147]. Matthew's Gospel says of Jesus: "But when he saw the multitudes, He was moved with compassion for them, because they were weary and scattered, like sheep having no shepherd. Then He said to His disciples, "The harvest truly is plentiful, but the laborers are few. Therefore pray the lord of the harvest to send out laborers into His harvest"[148].

This illustrates for us the compassion of the Lord, but also the need that there is for labourers to go out in His harvest and show the compassion of a shepherd. Jonah had been sent on just such a mission - to preach a message to a Gentile city burdened by sin. He was learning the need for compassion, just as the disciples were learning that need in their journeys with Jesus. The education of the disciples about compassion continued prior to, and during, the 'feeding of the five thousand' and the 'feeding of the four thousand', when Jesus said to them: "I have compassion on the multitude, because they have now continued with Me three days and have nothing to eat. And I do not want to send them away hungry, lest they faint on the way"[149].

Jesus' compassion was seen both in His dealings with the multitudes and also individuals, as shown in Mark 1: "Now a leper came to Him, imploring Him, kneeling down to Him and saying to Him, "If you are willing, you can make me clean." Then Jesus, moved with compassion, stretched out His hand and touched him, and said to him, "I am willing; be cleansed"[150]. From the writing of Peter we can see that the Lord had brought him to understand the importance of compassion.

Peter's surprisingly sympathetic tones show the development in his own life: "Finally, all of you be of one mind, having compassion for one another; love as brothers, be tenderhearted, be courteous; not returning evil for evil or reviling for reviling, but on the contrary blessing, knowing that you were called to this, that you may inherit a blessing".[151] In Old Testament and New, God is a God of compassion, and He teaches us how to practise it in our own lives, just as Jonah and the disciples learnt in their day.

CHAPTER TEN: JONAH – MISSION IMPOSSIBLE! (ALEX REID)

At the centre of the book of Jonah stand the words, "Salvation comes from the LORD"[152]. Many suggest that this is the main theme of the book, illustrating God's love to the Gentiles as well as His chosen people Israel. Yet the book of Jonah is as much about the man as the message. Jonah was a reluctant prophet, one who was angry at the success of his own preaching. An odd attitude indeed for a prophet of God. What improbable mission had God given Jonah to cause him to react in this way?

Jonah was instructed to preach against Nineveh the capital of the Assyrian empire, so why was he reluctant to obey? The problem, as far as the prophet was concerned, was the nature of the people he was instructed to preach to. The Assyrian empire of Jonah's day was a military superpower, whose battle tactics were of the most barbaric and brutal kind. Countless prisoners were cruelly slain in the course of Assyrian conquests; a kind of psychological warfare designed to cow their enemies. This aggressive military power was a real danger to Israel, a threat to her very existence.

Now that the wickedness of Assyria had come up before God[153], and they were ripe for judgement, would Jonah not have been happy to thunder out the judgements of God against such a cruel nation? It appears that he would have been glad to do just that if judgement was to be the outcome. But Jonah knew the nature of the God he served, a God who did not take pleasure in the death of the wicked[154], even a people as wicked as the Assyrians. Jonah knew that if Nineveh repented, God would forgive rather than judge, and Jonah wanted judgement.

Jonah stands in contrast to Abraham. When the outcry over the sin of the cities of Sodom and Gomorrah reached God and their impending judgement was revealed to Abraham, that man too knew the nature of the God he served, but appealed to that gracious nature that people might be spared[155].

It is strange that Jonah, who in his prayer from inside the great fish criticizes pagans for turning their backs on the grace of God[156], should wish to deny that grace to repentant sinners. Jonah seems to have harboured the idea that God's blessings should be restricted to Israel alone. Perhaps in our times Jonah would be called a racist and a bigot, someone whose personal prejudice was warping his appreciation of the grace of God. It seems incredible that the prophet was angry when God showed mercy to Nineveh[157]. His repeated requests to die show that he was wallowing in self-pity to the extent of defying God.

God challenged Jonah's anger and showed him how unwarranted his attitude was. In the incident of the vine God asked Jonah if he was right to be angry about the destruction of the plant. When Jonah claimed that he was justified, God contrasted his concern for an ephemeral plant with his indifference to the fate of at least 120,000 souls.[158] Could we be like Jonah in some of our attitudes? Is there a personal Nineveh we have to face up to? We may understand the import of the great commission to go into all the world[159], yet entertain thoughts that there are some groups of people who are not deserving of the grace of God, such as terrorists, suicide bombers and fanatics whose misdirected zeal causes so much pain. Or perhaps we are happy and secure in the knowledge of our own salvation, but feel no compunction to take the good news to others.

Perhaps the real lesson of the book of Jonah is that all our personal hang-ups, prejudices and self-centredness must be made subordinate to the will of God. Let us reflect on the fact that Jonah sat down to watch, hoping that the wrath of God would be poured out on a sinful city, but Jesus, outside another city, looked down from the cross to the end that the fountain of God's grace would flow out to a guilty world. Which attitude do we display?

CHAPTER ELEVEN: MICAH - CORRUPTION IN HIGH PLACES (BRIAN JOHNSTON)

Democratic countries elect their leaders. In other parts of the world where democracy hasn't taken a strong hold, international observers go to check if elections are more or less free and fair. We've seen that happen, and still there are squabbles in the aftermath. Often the losers cry 'foul'. The suspicion of corruption leaves a bad taste in the mouth. Non-elected leaders are removed by local military takeovers or in extreme cases by international efforts. Then comes the tricky business of handing back power to people who hold the respect of all factions – something that's far from easy. They say people get the leaders they deserve, but sadly, corruption seems inevitable.

Although the prophet Micah's message was directed at corrupt and oppressive leaders in Judah and Samaria in the eighth century BC, its principles are surely timeless and of broad application. It addresses the issue of the abuse of power. No abuse of power goes unobserved by the eye of God, and everyone – even to the greatest in the land – is accountable to God. So what did Micah have to say about it? In chapter three of his prophecy, he says:

> "Listen, you leaders of Jacob, you rulers of the house of Israel. Should you not know justice, you who hate good and love evil; who tear the skin from my people and the flesh from their bones; who eat my people's flesh, strip off their skin and break their bones in pieces; who chop them up like meat for the pan, like flesh for the pot."[160]

What a terrible indictment of leadership! The very ones who should have been protecting the people are described as cannibalizing them! Not feeding them, but fleecing them! Abraham Lincoln, the sixteenth president of the United States, said that it's not so much adversity that's a test of man's character as what he does when he's in a position of power. Here then were people in power who'd failed the test of character. The trouble was that it wasn't only the political leaders but the religious leaders as well. For Micah's condemnation continues:

> "This is what the LORD says: "As for the prophets who lead my people astray, if one feeds them, they proclaim 'peace'; if he does not, they prepare to wage war against him. Therefore night will come over you, without visions, and darkness, without divination. The sun will set for the prophets ..."[161]

The sooner the sun set on those prophets the better! They were in it for the money! It wasn't a divine vocation, simply a human profession. If someone fed them then they'd prophesy a peaceful or pleasant message for them; but if no generosity was shown, then that meant the message would be a hostile one! And sadly, even the priests were every bit as bad as the princes and prophets. Listen out for mention of them as Micah sums up all the corruption in high places at the end of his third chapter:

> "Hear this, you leaders of the house of Jacob, you rulers of the house of Israel, who despise justice and distort all that is right ... Her leaders judge for a bribe, her priests teach for a price ...Yet they lean upon the LORD and say, "Is not the LORD among us? No disaster will come upon us." Therefore because of you, Zion will be ploughed like a field, Jerusalem will become a heap of rubble, the temple hill a mound overgrown with thickets."[162]

Even the priests taught 'for a price'. God had designed their office to include the provision of instruction for his people.[163] But for these priests money was more important than God's truth – how tragic! Micah's message was not all gloom and despondency however. By the Spirit of God he was able to look far ahead and prophesy about a leader of true greatness who was coming. In the intervening time since Micah's prophecy in the eighth century BC that leader has come, but he will also come again. For it's Micah who gives us one of the great verses of Bible prophecy concerning 'the Christmas story' – and it's in this context of answering the need for a leader of stature. It's Micah who tells us that Jesus Christ was to be born in Bethlehem:

> "But you, Bethlehem Ephrathah, though you are small among the clans of Judah, out of you will come for me one who will be ruler over Israel, whose origins are from of old, from ancient times. Therefore Israel will be abandoned until the time when she who is in labour gives birth and the rest of his brothers return to join the Israelites. He will stand and shepherd his flock in the strength of the LORD, in the majesty of the name of the LORD his God. And they will live securely, for then his greatness will reach to the ends of the earth. And he will be their peace."[164]

This was the verse that wicked Herod was told about when he was looking to kill the child whose star had been seen by the wise men from the east. But it was to be thirty years later that Jesus Christ was killed, and it was no accident. The Bible tells us that: "It was fitting for [God] ... in bringing many sons to glory, to perfect[ly equip] the author [or chief leader] of their salvation through sufferings." (Hebrews 2:10 NASB). That's a reference to Jesus, the child who was born for the very purpose of dying. He died so as to become the great leader of our salvation. Sadly, two thousand years ago, the Jewish and Roman authorities didn't understand this when they put him to death. The Bible preacher charges them with the fact that they had:

> "... disowned the Holy and Righteous One, and asked for a murderer ... but put to death the Prince [or chief leader] of life, the one whom God raised from the dead, a fact to which we are witnesses."[165]

To have Jesus described as the chief leader of life is a wonderful description. His life here on earth was the best ever. He's the leading exponent of the art of living: the kindest and truest of men. And he has become, through his death on the cross, the source of new life: eternal life to each and every one of us who repents of our sins and fully trusts in him. Life in all its fullness which God wants us to enjoy is found in Jesus Christ – that's why God his Father raised up Jesus:

> "He is the one whom God exalted to His right hand as a Prince [or chief leader] and a Savior, to grant repentance ... and forgiveness of sins. [and the Bible preacher continues] ... we are witnesses of these things; and so is the Holy Spirit, whom God has given to those who obey Him."[166]

Jesus Christ says to us: "I am the Way, the Truth, and the Life."[167] If we're looking for purpose and direction in life, we need to follow the great leader whom God has appointed for us. This is what the Bible encourages his disciples to do - to:

"... run with endurance the race that is set before us, fixing our eyes on Jesus, the author [or chief leader] and perfecter of faith, who for the joy set before Him endured the cross, despising the shame, and has sat down at the right hand of the throne of God."[168]

That's what we mean when we say that Jesus Christ has come, but that he will also come again. He was born at Bethlehem, died at Jerusalem, is right now in heaven, and he's waiting to come back and take his rightful power and reign - just as Micah predicted to a world needing to see true and great leadership. Jesus' first coming was revealed to the shepherds, but when he comes next time he'll be the great shepherd of all his people, for Micah says:

"He will stand and shepherd his flock in the strength of the LORD, in the majesty of the name of the LORD his God. And they will live securely, for then his greatness will reach to the ends of the earth. And he will be their peace."[169]

He's the 'chief leader' – the greatest ever leader - who'll succeed in bringing peace and justice to this tired old world because he himself died to deal with its corruption. Let him lead you in life.

CHAPTER TWELVE: MICAH – NO CLUSTER (DAVID SMITH)

Micah felt keenly his isolation as he patiently walked the lonely path of obedience to God in a day of indifference and declension, a time when "the godly man is perished out of the earth", and discord and deceit were found on every hand.

Sitting in darkness while his enemies rejoiced against him, Micah looked to the Lord and waited for the God of his salvation, who more than 700 hundred years before had saved Israel out of the hand of the Egyptians.[170] With the intention of bringing them into the land of Canaan. He led them to Kadesh-barnea, from whence the twelve spies were sent to survey the promised land, "and they came unto the valley of Eshcol, and cut down from thence a branch with one cluster of grapes, and they bare it upon a staff between two ... that place was called the valley of Eshcol (a cluster), because of the cluster which the children of Israel cut down from thence."[171] Despite this evidence of the rich, fruitful place which God was going to give to His people, they there rebelled against him and murmured in their tents and said, "Because the LORD hated us, He hath brought us forth out of the land of Egypt, to deliver us into the hand of the Amorites. The people is greater and taller than we."[172]

Thus God was displeased with them and swore that they should not enter into his rest because of their unbelief.[173] But the day came when their children took possession of the land flowing with milk and honey given them by God, and with it went the divine guarantee that if they would hearken diligently unto the voice of the LORD their God, then blessings would come upon them and overtake them. But if they would not hearken unto the voice of the LORD nor keep His commandments then the LORD would smite the fruit of their ground and the labour of their hands, and although they planted vineyards and dressed them they would neither drink of the wine nor gather the grapes and the "olive shall cast its fruit."[174]

How sweet and satisfying to the soul of the godly is that which God provides for His own.' Surely Micah had often enjoyed the "first ripe fig"; it was something which his soul ever desired. It is of paramount importance to each one of us what our soul desires and how we satisfy that desire. Happy are they who can say like the Psalmist, "My soul longeth, yea, even fainteth for the courts of the LORD."[175] Such a longing desire is precious in the sight of God and blessed to behold in the life of saints, a resemblance to the Lord Jesus of whom it could be rightly said, "The zeal of Thine house shall eat Me up". The law and the testimony of the Lord are more to be desired "than gold, yea, than much fine gold"[176], even in this materialistic age.

Does it not become us to pray God to grant us an earnest desire for Him and His things that we may be able to say, "With my soul have I desired Thee ... diligently"?[177] Spiritual development is not possible in the life of a believer who has no desire for God and His word. Nothing can take the place of personal longing after God and continual feeding on His word. Peter says, "long for the spiritual milk ... that ye may grow thereby unto salvation."[178] Spiritual growth will come by no other means.

It is not surprising that the prophet should lament the prevailing sparseness, for well he knew that this was not mere misfortune but the hand of the Lord upon His people who had refused to hearken to His voice. The transgression of Jacob and the sins of the house of Israel were the cause of the dearth of the precious fruit of the land, and to Micah God had declared further foreboding judgement saying, "Yet shall the land be desolate because of them that dwell therein, for the fruit of their doings". It is sad that the people of the Lord by their evil doings could bring desolation to a land that once excelled in fulness and abundance as prepared by the Lord.[179] Surely these words are a solemn warning to all those to whom God has entrusted a divine heritage.

A depth of sorrow is expressed in Micah's words: "Woe is me! for I am as when they have gathered the summer fruits, as the grape gleanings of the vintage; there is no cluster to eat; my soul desireth the first ripe fig". The Israelite was commanded to leave the gleanings of his field and vineyard as a portion for the poor and the stranger. How moving that the faithful prophet through whom God had spoken concerning the coming to earth of His beloved Son, "whose goings forth are from of old, from everlasting"[180], should have no part among God's people but that of the poor and the stranger! Yet this is in keeping with the faithful of every age, "strangers and pilgrims on the earth", of whom the world is not worthy. But such an experience was a fellowship of the sufferings of the Christ and a shadow of the time when the true Prophet would come and find God's people Israel as barren spiritually as the fig tree that grew between Bethany and Jerusalem.[181]

No cluster (Heb. Eshkol) was available for Micah.[182] Once upon a time one cluster had to be carried between two men, now there was not sufficient for one man. Perhaps there are times when we also bemoan the lack of spiritual food in the assemblies. Week after week we find no cluster to eat but only the dried gleanings of the vintage. Sad indeed if there be no food in the Israel of God, nothing to raise the spirit and cheer the heart of God's people. Then well may we ask, is the cause of such famine due to our disobedience and indifference, and is God withholding his blessing till he sees a change in our hearts and an exercise in searching the Scriptures? Such famine can never be due to lack of divine resources, for through the Holy Spirit God can at any time work immeasurable blessing but often blessing is restrained through the negligence of His people. Lack of reading and meditation on the Scriptures will surely bring spiritual poverty. Diligent searching and conformity to God's word bring enriching blessing.

"Bring the whole tithe into the storehouse, that there may be meat in Mine house, and prove Me now herewith, saith the LORD of Hosts, if I will not open you the windows of heaven, and pour you out a blessing."[183]

Bible quotations from the Revised Version.

CHAPTER THIRTEEN: NAHUM – AN ANGRY GOD (DAVE WEBSTER)

"It shouldn't be allowed!" "They're a disgrace!" "What they did is unacceptable." You just turned on the radio or television and know at once that somebody is pretty angry about something!

The Rise and Fall of a Superpower

From obscure origins the Assyrians emerged to become the dominant power over seven hundred years from 1350 BC, bringing terror, war and oppression over a large area from Egypt to the Persian Gulf and north into Modern Turkey. Eventually establishing Nineveh as their capital, this arrogant, fierce and ruthless people terrorised its neighbours and brought fear into the small nations standing in their way. They destroyed Babylon, took out Damascus, shattered Samaria, bringing the Kingdom of Israel to an end, and conquered Thebes in upper Egypt. There seemed to be no stopping them.

Cruelty was their trademark. They were merciless; torturing, mutilating and murdering those they conquered. They invented a new policy forcing the people they conquered to migrate in large numbers to other areas of their empire. While they were at the height of their power Nahum came protesting at the violence, deploring the terror and, above all, declaring a message from God that they were finished! Within a short period of time, in 612 BC, the capital city of Nineveh was destroyed by the Babylonians, Medes and Scythians; and, by 609 BC, the Assyrian empire was completely overthrown.

Punishment

Nahum's message was of "a jealous and avenging God; the LORD takes vengeance and is filled with wrath. The LORD takes vengeance on his foes and maintains his wrath against his enemies."[184] But that anger was balanced with His love and kindness to those who trust Him: "The LORD is slow to anger and ... will not leave the guilty unpunished."[185] "... The LORD is good, a refuge in times of trouble. He cares for those who trust in him, but with an overwhelming flood he will make an end of [Nineveh]; he will pursue his foes into darkness."[186]

Why is God Angry?

"From you, [O Nineveh,] has one come forth who plots evil against the LORD."[187]

(1) Indignation! The people of Nineveh had experienced the mercy of God when Jonah had been sent with a call to repent which they had responded to.[188] That lesson had long been forgotten and yet God's judgment was delayed. There is good news and bad for us in this too: our God loves to forgive those who truly repent, but an old revival is no good to us if we have gone back to bad ways! As Paul put it: "Shall we go on sinning, so that grace may increase?"[189] It is fearful to think of God's attitude to nations which once embraced the Bible and feared God and who now enact laws and engage in practices which leave Him out of all their thoughts. It is an awful prospect to think of God saying "... you are vile."[190]

(2) Zero tolerance! The Assyrians were notorious for bloody and brutal conquests, inhumane treatment and demanding tribute for 'protection.'[191] God was not going to let them off with it. "Do not be deceived: God cannot be mocked. A man reaps what he sows."[192] So does a nation! The Assyrians, like so many today, gave no thought to accountability. The Bible assures us that "each of us will give an account of himself to God."[193] God does not tolerate evil today. The Lord Jesus paid the price to bring forgiveness: beyond that there is nothing but the bleak prospect of judgment.

(3) **Scandal!** Greed and exploitation characterised their trade – "You have increased the number of your merchants till ... like locusts they strip the land and then fly away."[194] Nahum cries out that morality and honesty have been neglected and the city was "... full of plunder, never without victims!"[195] The God who sees injustice in all its forms takes note and will act to redress this.

What Happened to Nineveh?

You just turn to the book of Nahum and know at once that somebody is pretty angry about something! Nahum is full of righteous indignation! God has the last word: "Nothing can heal your wound; your injury is fatal. Everyone who hears the news about you claps his hands at your fall, for who has not felt your endless cruelty?"[196]

Bible quotations are from the NIV.

CHAPTER FOURTEEN: HABBAKUK – A PROPHET FOR OUR TIMES (DAVID VILES)

We know nothing more about Habakkuk than his name, nor precisely when he wrote his prophecy. As chapter 3 implies that the temple was still functioning, the message must have been delivered before the fall of Jerusalem to the Babylonians (587/6 BC). Earlier, the description of conditions in Judah suggests a date during the chaos following the reforming King Josiah (died 609 BC). Somewhere between these dates Habakkuk found himself in a double-bind situation, familiar to many believers down the centuries - chronic internal disorder plus ominous threats from foreign influences over which the nation has no control.

Habakkuk's anguished cry of righteous indignation about the state of Judah opens the book[197] - violence everywhere, internal discord, widespread flouting of the law so that justice is perverted; these terms reflect Jeremiah's condemnation of the disastrous reigns of Kings Jehoahaz and Jehoiakim.[198] The prophet's reaction is to cry out (scream in pain or misery) against the breakdown of ordered society among God's people.

Habakkuk also perceives in the background ominous shifts in the great power balance; Judah must have been shocked by the news that all-powerful Nineveh had been destroyed[199] and the Assyrian army finally defeated at Carchemish in 605 BC. Carchemish is on the present-day Syrian/Turkish border, bringing to mind modern-day parallels with the situation confronting Habakkuk. In his time, Assyria was crushed by the thrusting, new top-dog regional power - Nebuchadnezzar, at the head of the formidable Babylonian war machine. God gives Habakkuk a graphic vision of just what was in store for Judah from the Babylonians - the hammer of the whole earth[200] - ruthless, impetuous, loving violence for its own sake, fierce, scornful, apparently unstoppable, a people who worshipped their own military prowess.[201] In our time, we may well feel that the state of our world is not dissimilar, with widespread crime and moral declension in society, and fear of real and uncontrollable violence, leading many to despair.[202]

What Is God Doing?

Habakkuk's consternation, then, is understandable, as ours might be as we struggle to reconcile experience of tragic, unpredictable events around us with trust in a loving, omniscient God. It is that trust, of course, which lies at the foundation of Habakkuk's worldview as it must do of ours. It is moving and instructive to trace how, as events appear to swirl uncontrollably around him, Habakkuk anchors himself firmly to what he knows experientially and doctrinally about God - the everlasting and holy one, the Rock of Israel, a God whose eyes are too pure to look on evil[203] - to try to make sense of what is happening. From this unshakeable basis of faith that God is in control and remains fully committed to His covenant people,[204] Habakkuk is emboldened in his agony of mind to question God:

"How long, LORD, must I call for help,

but you do not listen ...

but you do not save?[205]"

and then, apparently after the first shock of the Babylonian onslaught:

"Why then do you tolerate the treacherous?

Why are you silent while the wicked

swallow up those more righteous than themselves?"[206]

How can God allow such suffering to be inflicted by a godless people whose attitude to international relations is simple - destroying nations without mercy?[207]

These are basic, existential questions about human suffering which have preoccupied sensitive men and women of faith since at least the time of Job[208] and will do so until almost the end of time.[209] Our God is not unconscious of our yearnings, as is shown by His gracious responses to Habakkuk's faithful questioning.

The first response is not what the prophet expected, or to his liking, because God declares it is those very Babylonians whom He has appointed ... to execute judgement.[210] What is shocking about this - be utterly amazed, says the Lord, for I am going to do something in your days that you would not believe[211] - is that this judgment will also fall on Judah. Despite the fate which had already overtaken the northern kingdom, Jeremiah could accuse Judah in its rebellion and complacency of having lied about the LORD; they said, "He will do nothing! No harm will come to us; we will never see sword or famine."[212] A terrible disaster indeed was to befall them - a burden[213] of judgment for Habakkuk to proclaim to the people.

The second response is resoundingly important - echoes of Sinai are evoked as God instructs the prophet to inscribe the revelation on stone tablets to be heralded throughout the land.[214] This message is not to be ignored, and is as timely now as it was for Habakkuk and for all occasions when Christians are besieged by oppression or persecution: The LORD is in his holy temple; let all the earth be silent before him.[215] Despite appearances to the contrary, God is in control; He has ... determined that the people's labour is only fuel for the fire, that the nations exhaust themselves for nothing.[216]

Doesn't this put things into perspective and provide full reassurance that might is not right - that God's sovereign and unalterable purpose is to sum up everything in Christ?[217] Or, as Habakkuk puts it so majestically: The earth will be filled with the knowledge of the glory of the LORD, as the waters cover the sea.[218] Isaiah had spoken in similar but not identical terms;[219] Habakkuk's vision takes us further to focus not just on the knowledge, but on the knowledge of the glory of the Lord, to be revealed ultimately when every eye will see him and know Him among all the peoples of the earth.[220]

Meanwhile, God is not mocked;[221] tyrants great and small - whether Nebuchadnezzar, Suleiman, Pol Pot or the many others throughout history - will be held accountable for their barbarities and crimes. Written on Habakkuk's stone tablets in five woes[222] are some of the grounds upon which all unsaved people - tyrants or otherwise - will ultimately be deemed accountable, in deserved judgement;[223] pride, rapacity, self-aggrandisement, bloodshed, slavery and debauchery, humiliating others and idolatry - all these were indelibly inscribed as abhorrent to a holy God. A depressing list indeed, were it not for the one bright sentence to be inscribed with the rest - but the righteous will live by his faith.[224]

The Last Psalm

Habakkuk's prayer in chapter 3 is written as a psalm. Shigionoth (v.1) derives from a verb meaning 'to reel to and fro', reflecting the prophet's deep emotion after receiving such a powerful revelation. We use the word 'awesome' too superficially today, but it serves well to describe Habakkuk's reaction to what he had seen and heard.[225] His psalm, rooted historically in the mighty deeds wrought by God at the crossing of the Red Sea and the Jordan but informed by the awesome revelation he had just received, is in the form of a dramatic vision of God coming in martial power and glory with the armies of heaven - striding through the earth, threshing the nations in anger and delivering His people.[226] Habakkuk's concern is that this should happen quickly (Babylon fell to Cyrus the Great a few decades later[227]) but the psalm points us forward to a far greater and final victory when the Lord Jesus will return in the majesty of his power. [228]

Meanwhile, in view of this sure and certain hope, what should be our attitude to the darkening world around us and its increasingly oppressive impact on believers? Habakkuk puts it so beautifully in the doxology to his psalm which movingly expresses supreme confidence in the one who has promised never to forsake us[229]: though everything else fails, though the whole agricultural economy is blighted by the Babylonians, yet I will be joyful in God my Saviour.[230] No misplaced, unavailing optimism here, but a sure confidence in which we can share. It is based on our own personal experience of God's loving providence and the knowledge that the tension between continuing evil and injustice in the world and a compassionate, omnipotent God will be resolved at Christ's return as judge - for he must reign until he has put all his enemies under his feet. [231]

CHAPTER FIFTEEN: HABBAKUK - A BITTER PILL (BRIAN JOHNSTON)

Life's just not fair! That was the conclusion the Bible prophet was grappling with. His struggle is recorded in our Bibles because every generation faces the same challenge. Haven't we all been angered by examples of corruption or injustice in society? It was six hundred years before Christ when Habakkuk was facing up to this challenge. He spoke to God out of frustration: "How long, O LORD, must I call for help, but you do not listen? ... Why do you tolerate wrong? ... justice never prevails."[232]

He complained about a lot of things: violence, injustice, wrong, destruction, strife and conflict. His own people, the people of Judah in the south of the land of Israel, persisted in their wickedness despite his preaching, and it seemed to Habakkuk that God was letting them get away with it. God did answer His prophet, but not with the answer Habakkuk was expecting! "I am raising up the Babylonians ... a feared and dreaded people; they are a law to themselves and promote their own honour" (Habakkuk 1:5-9).

Surely the armies of the Babylonians weren't going to be God's instruments in dealing with his own people? That was even more of a problem for Habakkuk since he considered the Babylonians to be pagans, worse than even the most wicked among his own people! Habakkuk replied: "Your eyes are too pure to look on evil; you cannot tolerate wrong ... Why are you silent while the wicked swallow up those more righteous than themselves?"[233] Was God really going to let the Babylonians enhance their reputation at the expense of the Jews? Habakkuk now waits for God's answer. He describes this as standing upon his watch. The prophets were represented as being like watchmen positioned high on city wall or tower so they could see farther and bring warning to the city-dwellers.

When God's answer comes it brings with it the assurance that God is in overall control of history. The first reassurance that God gives his prophet is that His judgement is selective, knowing how to deliver the godly out of trouble. The proud Babylonians would come against Judah, but God would spare some. "See, he is puffed up; his desires are not upright - but the righteous will live by his faith."[234] This is the quotation of the Old Testament which Martin Luther made famous at the time of the Reformation. In the New Testament the words 'the righteous' - or the just – 'will live by ... faith' are applied to the salvation which believers on the Lord Jesus Christ possess.[235]

In the original setting here it could possibly describe one who believed what God had said about the Babylonian oppressors - as a result he would make his escape from the place, and save his life. But the believing Jew then is typical of all who wait for God's promises with patient faith, and so 'live' - or stand accepted - before God as a result. The Babylonian attacker, by contrast, though for a time executing God's judgments, at last becomes puffed up so as to attribute to his own power what is really the work of God - and by doing that he provokes God's displeasure. God's displeasure means that he too is going to be judged in his turn: "The cup from the LORD's right hand is coming round to you."[236]

God was going to use the Babylonians to teach his own people a lesson, but in doing so believing ones would be spared. Afterwards the cruel and wicked Babylonians themselves would be dealt with. The cup of God's anger and judgement would soon be passed to them to drink! When Habakkuk gets the point that God is in overall control, and that all wrongs are going to be dealt with in the broader sweep of history, he recalls how this has happened before in the history of God's dealings with his people: "in anger you threshed the nations. You came out to deliver your people, to save your anointed one. You crushed the leader of the land of wickedness, you stripped him from head to foot"[237], and so he says: "I will wait patiently for the day of calamity to come on the nation invading us."

And while he waits for God's judgements to catch up with the wicked, who are heedless of His longsuffering as their iniquity reaches its fullness, Habakkuk himself models the faith of the righteous man when he declares: "Though the fig-tree does not bud and there are no grapes on the vines ...? Yet I will rejoice in the LORD."[238] It's amazing how his conversation with God has dealt with all his frustration and left him trusting and joyful in God!

CHAPTER SIXTEEN: HABBAKUK – BRIBERY AND CORRUPTION (PAUL MERCHANT)

Every morning on my way to work I pass one of Edinburgh's cathedrals which stands between the Conan Doyle public house and a large John Lewis department store. A large banner hangs over the front door of the cathedral - 'Act justly, love mercy, walk humbly'. This challenging banner is a quotation from the prophet Micah. The brief, blunt words confront you like a shaft of light piercing the morning mist hanging low across Scotland's capital city. It is a salutary reminder for me as I approach another day's work.

Problems

Micah was a contemporary of Amos, Hosea and Isaiah and prophesied during the reigns of kings Jotham, Ahaziah and Hezekiah. He spoke out against bribery and corruption. He exposed the corrupt politics of the rulers and business men, "Her leaders judge for a bribe, her priests teach for a price, and her prophets tell fortunes for money."[239] "Both hands are skilled in doing evil; the ruler demands gifts, the judge accepts bribes, the powerful dictate what they desire - they all conspire together."[240]

Micah observed how bribery and corruption run through society like a broken sewer pipe down a street, seeping its pollution into every relationship, for "a son dishonours his father, a daughter rises up against her mother, a daughter-in-law against her mother-in-law - a man's enemies are the members of his own household."[241] Observing all this social and religious decadence was the God of Israel who had made promises, oaths and covenants regarding His chosen people. Micah knew the covenant obligations of the people of God and he yearned for his compatriots to exercise justice, peace and righteousness in their dealings with each other and in the laws of civil society. But he saw what was going on and saw that God would deal with his people. Micah was a man of God who knew how God deals with sin through the process of judgement, repentance, salvation, new life, hope.

"Therefore, the LORD says: 'I am planning disaster against this people, from which you cannot save yourselves. You will no longer walk proudly, for it will be a time of calamity.'"[242] Micah speaks the truth, but as a man of God he does not leave his countrymen without hope. He describes his God, "Who is a God like you, who pardons sin and forgives the transgression of the remnant of his inheritance? You do not stay angry for ever but delight to show mercy. You will again have compassion on us; you will tread our sins underfoot and hurl all our iniquities into the depths of the sea."[243]

Twice Micah refers to God in His shepherd, caring character.[244] He predicts that salvation will come through one to be born, and his prediction is this Shepherd would come from among the common people and deliver them from oppression and injustice and recover their right relationship with God. Micah was assured of this and displays his faith, "But as for me, I watch in hope for the LORD, I wait for God my Saviour; my God will hear me."[245]

The Great Shepherd

About 800 years later wicked king Herod had a verse from Micah quoted to him about the child Jesus whose star had been seen by the wise men from the east, "But you, Bethlehem Ephrathah, though you are small among the clans of Judah, out of you will come for me one who will be ruler over Israel, whose origins are from of old, from ancient times."[246]

Christ was revealed to the shepherds at His birth on the first occasion He came to earth. Next time He comes He will be the great Shepherd of His people, for Micah says, "He will stand and shepherd his flock in the strength of the LORD, in the majesty of the name of the LORD his God. And they will live securely, for then his greatness will reach to the ends of the earth."[247] Micah sees the Messiah - Christ - as the chief leader, the greatest ever leader who will succeed in bringing peace and justice to a corrupt world, because He died to deal with its corruption. From a nation riddled with bribery, corruption and dysfunctional family life, Micah predicts that the future reign of Christ will resolve the problems of this world. Until then, disciples of Christ are instructed not to offer the easy sacrifices of the wealthy, but rather to live out in their daily lives three simple commandments, "To act justly and to love mercy and to walk humbly with your God."[248]

Bible quotations are from the NIV.

CHAPTER SEVENTEEN: ZEPHANIAH – SEARCH ME, O GOD (ED NEELY)

Zephaniah's childhood survived Manasseh's wicked reign; his ancestry linked him to the reigning godly king Josiah. He probably prophesied during Judah's slight spiritual awakening before the destruction of Nineveh in 612 BC. Hilkiah, the priest, had discovered a copy of the Law and a renewed enthusiasm for the keeping of the Passover ensued. Why then was a prophet of the judgement of the day of the LORD so necessary? Because an indifferent and half-hearted people refused to grasp the warnings inherent in the captivity of her sister Israel and the present opportunities for godliness; she refused to seek the LORD or His righteousness, she neglected to seek humility and to abolish the worship of idolatry! Linked with his message of impending judgement flows the comforting reminder that even in the throes of what will be universal judgement remain the covenant mercies of a loving God. He will restore His people in millennial splendour even in the midst of righteous wrath. These two major themes of the prophecy and the attendant opportunities for acceptable service should have spurred the nation on to spirituality, but apathy and lethargy consumed the people and ultimate captivity must result. The things written beforehand are also written for our learning!

The term 'the day of the LORD' is used more frequently in this book than in any other Old Testament prophecy. That day, though perhaps mirrored in the captivity that would befall Judah, is a day yet future, for it will not appear until the man of sin is revealed, the son of perdition.[249] The Lord will be revealed from heaven with His mighty angels in flaming fire taking vengeance. How dare you and I adopt the same 'couch potato' attitude as prevailed among God's people Judah in

Zephaniah's day? There is a world around that is to be swept away, to be reduced to rubble, in Zephaniah's words, and you and I hold the words of life and prosperity. "The great day of the LORD is near; It is near and hastens quickly ... That day is a day of wrath, a day of trouble and distress, a day of devastation and desolation, a day of darkness and gloominess, a day of clouds and thick darkness ..."[250]

God is not indifferent to complacency. Zephaniah's great-great-grandfather had warned a priestly people many years before: "My sons, do not be negligent now, for the LORD has chosen you to stand before Him, to serve Him, and that you should minister to Him and burn incense."[251] Insipidness and stagnation, settling, "like the dregs of wine", complacency, are intolerable to God. "So then, because you are lukewarm, and neither cold nor hot, I will vomit you out of my mouth"[252] was God's up to the minute indictment of the nonchalant Laodicean church. Zephaniah 1:12 is current in its warning to the people of God.

God is neither inactive nor indifferent, either in judgement or in His willingness to search out and save. Running concurrent with Zephaniah's warnings of desolation and doom is the theme of comfort, consolation and restoration. He will restore His people in the future. "'I will leave in your midst a meek and humble people, and they shall trust in the name of the LORD ... they shall feed their flocks and lie down, and no one shall make them afraid."[253] Here, then, is the second compelling reason for Israel and all to serve Him. "Knowing, therefore, the terror of the Lord, we persuade men"[254]; "For the love of Christ compels us ..."[255]

Not only is judgement in righteousness assured, but also blessing in that same righteousness. The future holds great blessings for the nation that shall be "like the jewels of a crown, lifted like a banner over His land" (Zechariah 9:16), and even greater blessing for those who serve Him today. "Those who are wise shall shine like the brightness of the firmament, and those who turn many to righteousness like the stars forever and ever" (Daniel 12:3). And, "we shall be like Him, for we shall see Him as He is" (1 John 3:2).

Zephaniah means 'Jah has treasured'. He treasures His righteousness; He treasures His Word; He treasures His people. Our treasure should be there also, and where it is, there will our hearts be also.[256]

Bible quotations are from the NASB.

CHAPTER EIGHTEEN: HAGGAI – THE RESTORATION OF GOD'S HOUSE (STEPHEN HICKLING)

"Consider your ways!"[257]

Haggai's abrupt challenge to the remnant of God people in his day cuts to the heart with no less poignancy today. His message, directed at the people through Zerubbabel, their governor, and Joshua, their high priest, stirred them to action in the important matter of rebuilding the house of God, the temple in Jerusalem. As we together consider Haggai's message and its effect, we too should expect to have to stop what we are doing, to think and to re-evaluate our lives as the Spirit brings the relevance of its teaching to our hearts.

The book of Haggai has just two chapters, which comprise four short messages delivered over a four-month period in 520 BC. Why not read them now? Haggai, together with his contemporary, Zechariah, preached the need to finish the work of reconstructing the temple. It was a project that had lain dormant for some sixteen years since 536 BC, when the foundation had been laid by the first group of exiles returning home under the decree of King Cyrus following the fall of Babylon to the Medo-Persian Empire. Their resolve had been severely tested, though, by local opposition to the rebuilding and work had stopped. The response to Haggai's challenge was pronounced - the rebuilding of the temple was completed, in 515 BC, within just five years of their hearing the word of the Lord.

Rebuilding the House - What Relevance for Today?

You may be wondering how a 2,500-year-old rousing call to the physical work of reconstructing a ruined building has any bearing upon your disciple life today. Yet, as disciples of the Lord Jesus Christ in churches of God, we are engaged by the Lord as builders. The apostle Paul described himself as a wise master-builder, but his experience did not relate to the construction of physical buildings. What did he mean, then? Paul was in the business of building churches of God. He describes one such church, the church of God in Corinth, as 'God's building'[258] and as 'temple of God'[259] - not 'the' temple, but a microcosm of the larger whole. He later refers to that complete structure when he describes how each several building, fitly framed together, groweth into a holy temple in the Lord[260] - that is local churches of God combining to form the spiritual superstructure which answers to the temple of Haggai's day. As brothers and sisters in churches of God, we are engaged in nothing less than the work of building the spiritual house of God on earth today. This is not, in our day, a rebuilding from scratch; we are thankful to God for the building work of those who preceded us in that respect. It is, however, a work that must continue without ceasing, such that Haggai's word is no less relevant now than it was all those centuries ago.

Now is the Time!

"The time has not come, even the time for the house of the LORD to be rebuilt."[261]

So said the people of Haggai's day. Maybe the sentiment isn't wholly unfamiliar to you, whatever your stage in life. Perhaps you feel that now is the time to focus on your academic studies, or getting your first job, and you look forward to settling into stable employment - that will be the time to serve the Lord. For others, maybe it's the prospect of promotion, the home extension project, or the new car, which holds the attention. Or could it be that today is just 'family time'? Many of us look forward to a calmer, less frantic day in which we will have both energy and time to pour out in the Lord's things.

Still others will, no doubt, look back on days of faithful service in the house of God when the results of their labour were far grander than now. Their churches now seem like nothing in comparison[262] to their former glory. They hope that God will work wonders in the future, but don't expect them now.

God's instruction through Haggai was to "Go ... and rebuild ..."[263]; the Lord commanded his disciples to "Go ... and make disciples ..."[264] In his gospel, John records an occasion on which the disciples were concerned about food. The time was not right for outreach, in their view; their Master needed first to eat. Jesus said to them: "Do you not say, 'There are yet four months, and then comes the harvest'? Behold, I say to you, lift up your eyes and look on the fields, that they are white for harvest."[265]

The harvest time was at the fore of their minds - they expected it and dared not miss it. And whilst they properly waited its arrival, once the harvest came they knew that time was not on their side. Any delay would see the fruits of harvest lie upon the ground and rot; the harvest, when it arrived, would demand their undivided attention. But the Lord tells them of another harvest, which was already ripe, a harvest on which His attention was completely focused that day in Sychar. That same harvest of souls remains ready for reaping even now. Now is still the acceptable time; now is still the day of salvation[266]

What excuse will we give for delay in answering that simple command to go and make disciples, to build the house of God today? Will the Lord find us living in luxury,[267] while His house requires urgent maintenance?

Time to Re-evaluate Our Priorities?

To take pleasure in any of the things we have mentioned - our families, our homes, our jobs - would not appear to be wrong in itself. Isn't it just a matter of putting God at the top of our list of priorities? Not if our priority list is a list of equals! "You shall have no other gods besides Me." [268]

God doesn't want to be treated as number one in a list of other gods! In ordering our hearts, then, we must avoid allowing anything to take the seat of God, the hallowed place. His name alone is to be hallowed and we must strive to keep and, if necessary, to remove all else from the hallowed place in our lives. Adoration of God's holiness will ensure that other concerns take their rightful place.

How can we identify what occupies the hallowed place in our lives? We might start by considering what is important to us - our wallets and our diaries will give a reasonable indication of that. How do we spend our time and our money? A deeper examination might lead us to think about which things we look to for our joy. Our private prayer life may offer some clues. Do we pray only when something threatens our loved ones, our career or our possessions? Do we remain anxious about these things, even after we have prayed? Or are we regularly before God, prompted by our adoration of Him alone?

Israel had failed to give God His rightful place and, consequently, had neglected the work of the Lord. As a result, not only would they be the worse for failure to quench the real thirst of their souls for God, but they experienced a lack of satisfaction in material things too. Whether in food, in drink, in clothing or in wages, there was not enough to be satisfied.[269] Why? Because God withheld His blessing. More than that, He was actively taking away from the work of their hands until it resulted in a re-ordering of their hearts.

Conversely, when the people showed reverence for the Lord[270] and finished the work of rebuilding the temple, they experienced the Lord's blessing in material things too. The same principle applies today: "But seek first His kingdom and His righteousness, and all these things will be added to you."[271]

"Consider your ways," was Haggai's challenge to Israel. Similarly, the Lord Jesus challenged His disciples to 'consider the lilies',[272] which neither toil nor spin but which God clothes with royal finery. That thinking will set our hearts on God and on the things that He values and will result in renewed vigour for the work of building His house, which continues today.

Bible quotations from the NASB, unless otherwise stated.

CHAPTER NINETEEN: HAGGAI – BACK TO FRONT (MALCOLM MACDONALD)

Haggai is described as the 'Lord's messenger with the Lord's message'. We may think, "That's a great privilege"; but what if the message is a hard one to accept? Haggai had a bitter pill for the people to swallow, but thankfully they seemed willing to take it. There's a popular myth that the architect for the Glasgow Art Galleries made a fatal mistake in building it 'back to front'. The apocryphal story goes on to say that the architect chose death rather than face the consequences! As God's people we have serious issues to face in our day - we must pray for divine guidance lest we too fall into serious mistakes.

Because of external factors the people had ceased the rebuilding of the temple after the return from Babylon. The excuse given was that it was not the time for the house to be rebuilt. It's not hard for us to give the same excuse for not doing things for the progress of God's work. There are many reasons we could give for not doing this or that for the progress of the gospel and the truth. Does our failure to do these things only serve to give us more time to do our own things?

Such reasonings are not hidden from God. He challenges the people, "Is it a time for you yourselves to be living in your panelled houses, while this house remains a ruin?"[273] This question should cause heart-searching with us all. The matter of our time management is perhaps crucial to the whole of our disciple walk. When the Lord spoke to some men in Luke 9, they all had some reason why it was not suitable at that time for them to follow Jesus.

Here is the first consideration the Lord asks them to think about.

- They had sown but hadn't reaped

- They had eaten but were still hungry

- They had drunk but were still thirsty

- They were clothed but were still cold

- They had been paid but were still poor

These were serious things that were wrong with the people of God. The second consideration from the Lord put a challenge to them: "Go up into the mountains and bring down timber and build the house, so that I may take pleasure in it."[274] He underlines this consideration with a solemn reminder of the disappointments they had experienced because God's house lay in ruins and they were all busy building their own fine homes. Luke tells us the only thing recorded about the Lord Jesus from early childhood to manhood was "Why were you looking for me? Did you not know that I must be in my Father's house?"[275] In this short prophecy of Haggai we read more than 20 times of God's house. If it occupied the attention of the Lord to such an extent should it not occupy us to the same extent?

Haggai's call to action brought a welcome response, first from the governor of Judah, then from the high priest and, finally, from the entire remnant, who came and worked on the house of the Lord of hosts. Their spirits had been touched and that made all the difference. Even though they were engaged in a far smaller work than that of their forefathers, yet they had caught the vision that this thing was for God. The answering call from the throne of heaven to this people with hearts that had been touched was one that brought strength to the people. "Be strong, O Zerubbabel ... Be strong, O Joshua ... Be strong, all you people of the land."[276] What a difference to a people who previously had been doing things 'back to front'. It wasn't an easy come-back. Hard work was required then to reverse a negative trend. The same is still true today if we are to see divine blessing among us.

Once more the prophet asks the people to consider. Before they thought to lay a stone for the temple they were being impoverished. After the foundation stone was laid and things were left unfinished, they were still impoverished. But here comes the divine promise, "From this day on I will bless you."[277] Would they believe the promise of their God? Our God is still waiting to bless us.

Bible quotations from the NIV, unless otherwise stated.

CHAPTER TWENTY: ZECHARIAH – THE COMING KING (DAVID VILES)

"Who despises the day of small things?"[278]

For the most quoted prophet in the New Testament, we know very little more about Zechariah than his name. Elsewhere, this name always appears coupled with that of his contemporary, Haggai - they prophesied to the Jews who were in Judah and Jerusalem, in the name of the God of Israel, who was over them.[279] They spoke at a particularly low time in the history of God's chosen people, reduced to a rump of chastened returnees from Babylon in 538 BC with, nevertheless, big ideas for rebuilding the temple of the Lord. Eighteen long years later, local and official opposition had taken its toll; 'small things' had been accomplished - the temple foundations were finished - but optimism had been replaced by demoralisation and the pressure of competing priorities.

Into this unpromising context God sent His two prophets to uplift and inspire. While Haggai gave practical encouragement for governor Zerubbabel and high priest Joshua, with tempting glimpses of what that temple will be in a future day, Zechariah soars in a series of vivid, poetic visions and revelations across the length and breadth of the earth's geography and history, past, present and future. The immediate issue, completion of the rebuilding of the temple, will be accomplished - that is the unalterable purpose of the sovereign Lord: "I am returning to Jerusalem with mercy; My house shall be built in it."[280] Zechariah draws attention repeatedly to the divine choice of Jerusalem as the place of God's Name;[281]

God cannot forget the covenant bond – "They shall be My people and I will be their God" - nor the imperative to uphold the honour of His holy Name.[282] It is as if, after centuries of disobedience and 70 years of exile, God can no longer bear the estrangement of His people - "I am very jealous for Zion; I am burning (ardent) with jealousy for her."[283] Central to Zechariah's message for God's people is the fact that a new era is dawning.[284] On their part, in response to God's restoring grace, His people are to cultivate fruits worthy of repentance, pursuing justice, mercy, compassion, truth and peace, and avoiding that which God hates.[285]

Jerusalem - a Home Fit for a King

But the immediate issue does not define the limits of Zechariah's message. Looming beyond to encourage the remnant in their endeavours is the glorious vision of Jerusalem as the millennial centre of the earth. Preceded by the apocalyptic events of 'the Day of the Lord' related in chapters 9 to 14, Jerusalem will become the focus of all nations seeking the Lord as prophets had promised years before. A day will come when 'ten men from every language of the nations shall grasp the sleeve of a Jewish man, saying, "Let us go with you, for we have heard that God is with you."'[286] This must have astounded the struggling temple builders of Zechariah's day.

How many of them would have recalled the solemn words of Psalm 2 - "Yet I have set My King on My holy hill of Zion. '... Ask of Me, and I will give You the nations for Your inheritance.'"?[287] The new era is to set the stage for the glorious appearing of God's King. Leapfrogging the millennia, Zechariah challenges little Jerusalem with the vision of ultimate peace and concord centred on a city which has become so extensive that it will burst its walls as the nations flock to worship;

and, because the Lord 'will be the glory in her midst,' [288] the acme of contentment for His people will at last prevail with everyone inviting 'his neighbour under his vine and under his fig tree. '

This King will unite the offices of governor and priest, for so long separated in the purposes of God. Through vivid and direct messages and visions, God encourages governor Zerubbabel to complete the rebuilding of the temple and high priest Joshua to own the holiness of his role;[289] but in one poetic and mysterious vision Zechariah presents two anointed ones who together stand beside the Lord of the whole earth, jointly supplying the oil to keep alight the lampstand of divine testimony. The immediate purpose is to give encouragement to both individuals as they together play out their separate roles. However, beyond that we can discern the One who is for us both King of kings and great High Priest and who supplies to each of us the Spirit and through the Spirit the basis of our corporate testimony as He moves in the midst of the golden lampstands.[290]

The Servant King

While Zechariah was inspired with visions of a future lying far beyond him in the King's millennial reign, he was also privileged to discern aspects of the King which, though future to him, are now treasures for us from the life of the Lord. It is notable that many of the references to Zechariah's words in the New Testament are used to point to, or amplify, events in the final passion week of the Lord's life. As well as the Lord high and lifted up in glory, he foresees the Christ who was made a little lower than the angels, for the suffering of death.[291]

Two images in particular, well known from earlier prophets, are taken up and developed in Zechariah's writings. "Behold, I am bringing forth My Servant, the Branch" - the same word is used by Jeremiah to describe the 'shoot' of King David, who will reign and judge with righteousness.[292] Zechariah's contribution is, like Isaiah's in chapters 52 and 53, to couple the thought of the kingly Branch with the concept of the Servant of God and to emphasise again that this King will be both ruler and priest on His throne - so that "the counsel of peace shall be between them both."[293] The second familiar image is that of the Shepherd of Israel and the contrast He offers with the false and worthless shepherds who care only to exploit the flock for their own gain. Like Ezekiel before him, Zechariah describes in excoriating terms the fate of those 'shepherds'[294] and presents aspects of the Good Shepherd who will bring back His flock "as though I had not cast them aside."[295] Although the context here is primarily millennial, there are heart-warming insights into our kingly Shepherd which shine out like gems. We are told, half a millennium before it happens, that this Shepherd will indeed be betrayed for 30 pieces of silver, the price of a slave, which will be thrown for the potter;[296] and we are riveted by the statement "Awake, O sword, against My Shepherd, against the Man who is My Companion, " says the LORD of hosts. This kingly Shepherd stands alongside God and yet it pleased the LORD to bruise Him ...[297]

There is one other incident in the passion week of the King which is presaged uniquely by Zechariah; it is one of the few incidents from His life which is referred to by all four Gospel writers, Matthew and John directly referring back to the prophet.[298] The coming of Messiah riding on a donkey was plainly a scripture well-known to expectant Jerusalem at the time, and the qualities highlighted in this King - of justice, having salvation and lowliness - were as attractive then as they are to the Christian today. Shouts of joy are to accompany His arrival because, "I am coming and I will dwell in your midst ... many nations shall be joined to the LORD in that day", yet on that day His ancient people "will look on Me whom they pierced."[299] Once again, the millennia conflate and merge in Zechariah's visions as he tells of the King who "shall speak peace to the nations " and whose "dominion shall be from sea to sea." [300]

Bible quotations from the NKJV, unless stated otherwise.

CHAPTER TWENTY-ONE:
ZECHARIAH – WHAT DO YOU SEE?
(DAVID SMITH)

A remnant had returned from Babylon to rebuild the house of God in Jerusalem, but after some conflict with their adversaries the work had ceased. The urgency to recommence was lost sight of until God raised up Haggai and Zechariah, prophets to instruct and encourage the people to start again, and so fulfil the prime purpose of their return.[301] It was then, as it is now, God's intention that His house should be built by men, according to a divine pattern.[302] To help forward this work is a blessed privilege.

In God's disclosures to Zechariah, there are visions and parables, some of which are hard of interpretation but profound in spiritual meaning. There is a foreshadowing of events that are yet future, in particular involving the people of Israel and the advent and acknowledgement of their Messiah, the Lord Jesus Christ. On one occasion Zechariah was wakened by an angel who said to him "What seest thou?" And he said, "I have seen, and behold, a lampstand all of gold, with its bowl upon the top of it, and its seven lamps thereon ... and two olive trees by it."[303]

While the prophet was unable to interpret the meaning of the vision, it was not difficult to recognize the "lampstand all of gold," although there was an alteration in design. For six hundred years a similar lampstand had been an important piece of furniture in God's dwelling place. It was made of one piece of pure gold, speaking, we suggest, of the divine character of our Lord Jesus Christ, who was one with the Father, "being the effulgence of His glory, and the very image of His substance."[304]

The functioning of the lampstand depended on the children of Israel bringing "pure olive oil beaten for the light, to cause a lamp to burn continually.[305] When the sun set over the desert horizon and the day gave place to darkness, inside the tabernacle the lamps burned before the Lord with the oil which the Israelites had brought. It lit up the table of showbread which presented to the Lord the twelve tribes in the twelve loaves of bread. Without the beaten oil darkness would have prevailed. Blessed ministry indeed to supply the fuel for the light in God's house. Well did the Psalmist say, "As for me, I am like a green olive tree in the house of God;" only an olive tree growing quietly in the background, but vital to the service of God's house. What more noble work can one ever aspire to than to bring the oil for the light of divine testimony? When the Holy Spirit is allowed to operate in the lives of the saints then are the beauties of Christ manifest and every gift ministered in the grace of God; beaten oil indeed of a very high value!

The lampstand was not exclusively an Old Testament vessel, but appeared significantly in the vision of the apostle John on the isle of Patmos. He saw seven golden lampstands, each representing a church of God then extant in Asia.[306] The New Testament teaches us that every believer who has come to Christ is lightened by the "light of life"[307] and is sealed by the Holy Spirit. They are "light of the world," not to be hid under a bushel but to be put "on the stand."[308] It is sad that many dear believers disregard the will of the Lord that they should be placed on a lampstand, that is, in a church of God according to the pattern of Scripture, and so joined with others to burn brightly for the truth of God in a world of increasing darkness.

What do you see? Fellow-believer, do you see a lampstand as a church of God today, fed with pure olive oil produced from within, not by craft or ability, "not by might, nor by power, but by My Spirit?" As we allow the Holy Spirit to operate in our hearts and to form in us the likeness of Christ, so shall we be to His praise and glory and so shall the light of divine testimony burn radiantly.

Bible quotations from the Revised Version.

CHAPTER TWENTY-TWO: MALACHI – THE PROPHET WITH A WAKE-UP CALL (GILBERT GRIERSON)

It was the preacher in Ecclesiastes 3 who said that there is "a time to keep silence and a time to speak."[309] Malachi was raised up by God to speak to the nation of Israel in a period of declension, and he could not keep silent but speak out the "oracle (or "burden", RV) of the word of the Lord."[310] This was to be the last word from God to His chosen nation for about 400 years until the coming of the "messenger of the covenant",[311] the Lord who would be like "a refiner's fire" and "purifier of silver"[312] to purify and refine His people so that their offerings would be pleasing to God again.

Again? So was God not finding pleasure in His people? No! Far from it! These were dark days in Israel's history; days of nominal service, cold hearts and blind eyes. Malachi prophesied to Judah after their return from Babylon, which took place in successive stages over roughly a century, starting at approximately 536 BC. The Northern Kingdom as an entity, who had previously been known as 'Israel', did not return from Assyrian exile; the remnant of Judah who came back from Babylon are now described as 'Israel'.[313] The remnant here was the small number of faithful Jews of all tribes who responded to God's call to return from captivity.

Is the prophecy just a message for its own time? In Galatians 6:16, God's new covenant people, made up of Jews and Gentiles is described as "the Israel of God." So we listen to see if it is relevant in our own time, too, and to each one of us personally.

The format of Malachi's prophecy is a dialogue between God and His people. In response to God's words to them, they had many questions and God answers them. The Spirit of God, speaking through Malachi, was able to assess and diagnose the condition of the hearts of the people, and the questions they asked reflected the low state into which they had fallen. God's desire was to bring about repentance and revival - needed then, and now, if we are honest!

"I have loved you" was God's opening statement, and how hurtful to Him to hear the people's reply, "How have you loved us?"[314] They had been chosen by God over Esau in sovereign grace to fulfil God's purposes, and it had not been because of anything commendable in them. Nothing could frustrate God's plans. Esau's descendants who formed the nation of Edom, despite their resistance, would be judged by God for their sin against Israel and cease. (Visit the ruins of Petra in Jordan for graphic proof of God's faithfulness in keeping His word in chapter 1, verse 4.)

How reassuring to us today to know that we who, by grace, have been chosen in Christ "before the foundation of the world"[315] have a God who is a covenant-keeping God. Even if we are faithless, He remains faithful to His own character and purpose; that's the nature of our great God.[316] But Israel could not see all of this; they had forgotten God's covenant promises and based their judgement on the prevailing circumstances of the time. As a small remnant, they felt their weakness. So how could God be for them? They needed their eyes to be opened!

Malachi had a hard message from God for the priests. God said that they despised His name. "How have we despised your name?" was their reply.[317] It was evident in the quality of their offerings. Far from giving their best they brought the blind, lame and sick animals as sacrifices. Did they think God couldn't see? What they gave reflected the value they had put upon the person to whom they gave. No wonder God was offended.

How much time and effort do I put into my offerings of praise and worship? Are they truly 'sacrifices'? And does my weekly giving to the Lord reflect a heart that is truly grateful for all He has poured out for me? Am I giving my best? Guy Jarvie, writing in NT magazine in 1948, said about Israel in Malachi's day, "Positionally, they were at the place, but conditionally, alas, they were far away in heart."[318] This is an ever-present danger for God's people.

If the priests did not repent and reform they would be cursed; in fact, God had already cursed them, by withdrawing blessings.[319] In chapter 2:4-7 God paints the picture of what He looked for in Levi, with whom He had made a covenant. A priest was to fear and reverence God, give true instruction, speak truth, walk "in peace and uprightness" (12) turn many from iniquity, guard knowledge, and seek instruction from God. God's ideals are very high but He has not lowered the bar for His priests today. That humbles me, as the Spirit of God searches my heart to reveal how far short I often fall!

In chapter 2, Malachi tells Israel that they had wearied God with their words. And when they protested, "How have we wearied him?", his answer was that they were accusing God of delighting in evil doers and being unjust.[320] They were making serious charges against God!

But not all received God's condemnation, and we read in chapter 3 that there were still some - a remnant of a remnant we might say - who "feared the Lord", who "spoke with one another."[321] God knew, and had a book of remembrance written with their names. They were His personal possession, and he would spare them "as a man spares his son who serves him."[322] It would be very clear in a future day whom the righteous and the wicked were! The day will declare it.

The book of Malachi closes with the announcement of that future day, a day of judgement for the wicked but "for you who fear my name, the sun of righteousness will rise with healing in its wings."[323] His announcement of the coming Messiah, the One who would "suddenly come to his temple"[324] should have had the effect of causing the people of God to repent, to turn their spiritual eyes upward and to look expectantly and wait (like Simeon in Luke 2) for "the consolation of Israel" and this promised "sun of righteousness" who would come to heal them of their sins by His wounds received at Calvary.[325]

"How shall we return?" the people had asked God in chapter 3. This was in answer to God's loving commandment, "Return to me and I will return to you, says the LORD of Hosts."[326] Unbelieving Israel, as a nation, have still not returned and have yet to repent and receive Him whom they despised and rejected.[327] That day will come! "What will their acceptance mean but life from the dead?"[328] On that day the prophesy in Malachi chapter 4:2-3 will be fully realised. What joy!

In conclusion, there is nothing 'minor' in Malachi's prophecies! His themes include God's sovereignty, God's amazing love, His inevitable judgement against sin and assessment of Israel's condition with hard, searching words for the priests, a passionate call to get right with God, and to "bring the full tithe into the storehouse."[329]

John Blanchard in his book on the minor prophets, wrote, "It is possible to read Malachi in less than ten minutes - but it is impossible to read it comfortably, as its message is as powerfully disturbing now as when it was first written."[330] Today also we must not keep silent; it's a time to speak. God burdened His prophet Malachi with a timely message. His name translates as 'my messenger'. The apostle Paul was burdened in his day with God's message of salvation for all who would believe. His burden was "to testify to the gospel of the grace of God."[331] Are we burdened today to pass the message on?

Malachi, the last book in our Old Testament, contains a vital message from God to Israel. At the close of our New Testament scriptures we hear the apostle John's exhortation to disciples of the Lord Jesus Christ which is still vitally important today: "And now, little children, abide in him, so that when he appears we may have confidence and not shrink from him in shame at his coming. If you know that he is righteous, you may be sure that everyone who practices righteousness has been born of him."[332]

Bible quotations from the ESV.

CHAPTER TWENTY-THREE:
MALACHI – ROBBING GOD!
(DAVID VILES)

Malachi - a Message for Our Times

Scripture provides few clues to the context of Malachi's message. Clearly, he was writing some time after the events narrated by Ezra and (possibly) Nehemiah, when the fervour surrounding the rebirth of the nation and its worship following the return from Babylon was already a distant memory. Times were relatively easy; Israel was entering its long waiting period for the promised Messiah. To those who remained faithful, revering the Lord's name, was promised the sight of "the sun of righteousness [that] will rise with healing in its wings".[333] But for many, and particularly the leaders of the nation, fervour and faith had been replaced by weariness and cynicism. The prevailing moral and spiritual tone is reminiscent of the 'scoffers' of our age – "Where is this 'coming' he promised?"[334] Neglect of God and of His priorities was leading to pernicious spiritual and moral decline. Does any of this sound familiar?

Spiritual Decay

The structure of Malachi's message - an extended dialogue between God and His people - is unique to this prophet. The questions which Malachi attributes to the people may have represented their unspoken thoughts, but they went to the heart of the national spiritual malaise: robbing a loving God of His due and in the process robbing themselves of the joy of the covenant.

"How have you loved us?"[335]

What a breathtaking question! But it can and does still happen - we have it on divine authority - that our love may grow cold.[336] As rank godlessness increases in our cultures, so may robbing God through ingratitude and wilful neglect of our reasonable service[337] in response to God's covenant love. Failure to strive daily to become rooted and established in love[338] will lead inevitably to a life which is spiritually withered and blasted. It's that basic!

"How have we shown contempt for your name?"[339]

One of God's names is 'Jealous'.[340] Sadly, it was the priests who were giving the lead in robbing God by despising it. 'Harsh things' were being said about that name - such as the futility of serving the Lord if it meant being different from the world.[341] Like many others today, God demands respect[342] - and disciples hardly need reminding that friendship with the world is enmity with God.[343]

"How have we defiled you?"[344]

Well, it was barefaced robbery! Withholding of the tithe, and the offering of crippled, blind animals for sacrifice to the Lord of creation, drew from God words of utter condemnation of their "useless fires on my altar."[345] Better no worship at all than sacrifices like these. For us today, this extreme example forces very personal and searching questions - what priority are we prepared to give to serving God and to the quality of that service? "If Jesus Christ be God and died for me, then no sacrifice can be too great for me to make for Him."[346]

Post-Christian Morality

Many contemporary pundits propound the view that western societies have outgrown the need for God. But without Him, there is no need for moral absolutes - the 'rightness' of what we do is relative only to the effects it has on ourselves or on wider society. There is nothing new about this; in Malachi's society, as in ours, the process of robbing God leads inexorably to the results we see today - men and women robbed of the peace and fulfilment of living in acknowledgement of personal accountability to God.[347]

"Why do we profane the covenant of our fathers by breaking faith with one another?"[348]

Although that covenant had been with God, the responsibilities of each to his neighbour had been clearly stated[349]. Leave God out of the equation and the result was - and is - the cult of the individual. Sorcery, perjury, defrauding and oppression are some of the malign results enumerated by Malachi[350] - we can add many more.

"Why?"[351]

There was no obvious blessing from God, despite the crocodile tears of restored Israel.[352] God focuses a searching light on the reason - faithlessness in marriage relationships. "I hate divorce"[353] is an unequivocal statement, by God, as relevant in today's social conditions as then. The social consequences of divorce are painfully evident in the spread of dysfunctional family relationships throughout western society, robbing children and adults alike of the security and fulfilment of loving family life as God intended it. Malachi also highlights the return of the old sin of intermarriage with the surrounding peoples, bringing 'foreign gods' into the home environment.[354] The frequency and the vehemence with which the Old Testament addresses this practice[355] surely emphasise the force of Paul's injunction to our own time not to be yoked together with unbelievers, in marriage as in other relationships.[356]

"Where is the God of justice?"[357]

Speaking through His prophet, God highlights the ultimate consequence of this process of declension - an inversion of moral values, whereby wicked conduct is praised and the arrogant admired.[358] With no sense of accountability to God, and no reliable inbuilt moral compass, justice is perverted and the poor and the weak are left to go to the wall. It's all as fresh as tomorrow's newspaper headlines!

"How are we to return?"[359]

Some, at least, of Malachi's contemporaries were asking this question. The answer was the same as it ever was, and is now – "'Return to me and I will return to you," says the LORD Almighty'.[360] Instead of robbing God and devouring each other there is held out an amazing promise – "See if I will not throw open the floodgates of heaven and pour out so much blessing that you will not have room enough for it". [361] The challenge for us as disciples comes earlier in the verse: "Bring the whole tithe into the storehouse, that there may be food in my house."

Bible quotations are from the NIV.

BONUS BOOK: MUSINGS ON THE MINOR PROPHETS (LES HORNE)

CHAPTER ONE: HOSEA – "AS THEY CALLED THEM, SO THEY WENT FROM THEM"

There is thunder in the air. All through the Minor Prophets there is a feeling of storm. Occasionally the clouds break and the sun shines with a promise of summer, and then they roll up again, heavy with failure, and ingratitude and hatred, to hide God's mercy and grace.

There are twelve prophets after Daniel. They are called the Minor Prophets, but the only "minor" thing is the quantity of their writing that has been preserved for us. Their messages are emotional and outspoken, the voice of God with a throb in it. They were speaking in a world that was disintegrating around them. Sometimes the cracks were hidden by social prosperity but the eye of God could see the trembling structure behind. They were crying out warnings in a desperate world that faced famine, disease and violence, a morally rotten world, and because their situation was like ours, their messages are particularly meaningful to us. Occasionally they wrote in riddles; some of their messages were concerned with contemporary events that have no immediate significance for us; and we find the intense, figurative language different from the matter of fact, earthbound prose of our daily reading, but there are things that God says through them that He says nowhere else with such emphasis. We must read them.

Hosea started to prophesy in the 8th century B.C. He was contemporary with Jonah, Amos and Joel, and probably Micah, and a little before Isaiah, Jeremiah and Obadiah. Malachi was the last of the Old Testament prophets and was probably preaching in the time of Nehemiah, about 430 B.C. The total span is about 300 years and the area in which the prophets lived was the northern and southern kingdoms of Israel and Judah. This three hundred years covers the fall of Samaria, the fall of Jerusalem, and the rebuilding of the temple and the city. In the same period Assyria crumbled, Nineveh fell, and the empire of Babylon was conquered by the Persians. A hundred years after Malachi, Alexander of Macedon was in Jerusalem. It was three hundred years of turbulence.

I would like to take you through the landmarks in the Minor Prophets, not as an exhaustive study but like a guide, noting some points of special interest that, to use a guidebook phrase, "must not be missed". I would like you to feel the passion of God's voice as He called to His people, called to their backs because they were going away from Him. I would like you to see the very ordinary men with the extraordinary messages who shared the task of standing up for God in the developing chaos:

> "O Jerusalem, Jerusalem, which killeth the prophets, and stoneth them that are sent unto her! How often would I have gathered thy children together, even as a hen gathereth her own brood under her wings, and ye would not!" (Luke 13:34).

Hosea was the first, perhaps not in time but in the order in which the books were arranged. Amos may have been a few years before him and it is most probable that they knew of each other because Amos did not hide his light. Hosea was a native of the Northern kingdom. His story is an unhappy one. In obedience to God's call, he married a wife named Gomer who had a reputation for immorality, Gomer bore three children before she left Hosea for other lovers. In chapter three, Hosea recounts how he found her in slavery and bought her back to himself.

There are many questions that are raised by the story of Hosea. It seems strange that God should have involved His servant in such an unsatisfactory relationship. Hosea is not alone in being asked to perform strange acts. Isaiah had to walk naked (Isaiah 20:2), and Ezekiel had to eat dung (Ezekiel 4:12). Hosea's experience was only a part of the involvement of God in history. It was not an isolated little parable, artificially staged for the benefit of others. Often God's servants suffer from the effects of moral corruption and spiritual blindness that poison the environment we live in, but they never suffer more than God suffered, or are as deeply involved in the catastrophe of sin as He is.

Hosea learned how sin spoiled the relationships of people, how it destroyed the joy of life. He learned the cost of loving somebody who was continually unfaithful, and the real, practical meaning of grace. His message has been described as "the gospel according to Hosea". Out of his experience, he talked with knowledge about "hesed", the steadfast love that is a moral bondage. He described God's relationship to His people in those terms (Hosea 2:12), and he asked that their relationship to Him should be of the same quality (Hosea 6:6). But all the grace and love was ignored and it only provides a background for a picture of sin. "When Israel was a child, then I loved him, and called My son out of Egypt. as they called them, so they went from them" (Hosea 11.1). "But God, being rich in mercy, for His great love wherewith He loved us ... quickened us," as Paul says to the Ephesians, and grace does not rest easy, it moves out into the desert in search.

Hosea learned to carry the burden of the lost, of the unlovely and unholy. He bore the burden of Gomer's shame: "Go yet, love a woman beloved of her friend and an adulteress, even as the LORD. loveth the children of Israel, though they turn unto other gods." In Isaiah there is a passage of equal pathos: "Bel boweth down, Nebo stoopeth; their idols are upon the beasts, and upon the cattle: the things that ye carried about are made a load, a burden to the weary beast. They stoop, they bow down together; they could not deliver the burden, but themselves are gone into captivity. Hearken unto Me, O house of Jacob, and all of the remnant of the house of Israel, which have been borne by Me from the belly, which have been carried from the womb: and even to old age I am He, and even to hoar hairs will I carry you" (Isaiah 46:1-4).

The burden of grace and forgiveness is not easy to carry. Hosea bore it. God bears it. But we carry grudges and prejudices and refuse to help people who hurt us and fail people who need us because they do not come to us and we will not go to them. There is not, in all the Bible, a more wonderful statement of God's love than the message of Hosea. It is charged with emotion to the last chapter, where he pleads with Israel to say, "Neither will we say any more to the work of our hands, Ye are our gods: For in Thee the fatherless findeth mercy. I will heal their backsliding, I will love them freely" (Hosea 14:3,4).

The experiences of Hosea lend power to his words as he speaks of the intense longings of God for His people to leave the petty interests and the involvement with the worship of material things for the experience of real life in the glory of His presence. We do not know whether the relationship between Gomer and Hosea survived, whether the faithless woman warmed to the grace of her true lover and responded to his forgiveness. We know how Israel failed to respond to the love of God and what the consequences were. We know how the loving kindness of God is directed to another people now, and the statement, "I am God, and not man; the Holy One in the midst of thee" (Hosea 11:9), should be very meaningful to you and me. When God was in the midst of Israel, they turned away to little blocks of gold and carved granite, to hand-carved cedar figures with bulging eyes. Their gods failed them then as ours fail us now, security and comfort, fine houses, safe investments and status, success in business, social acceptance and scholastic achievement, all the little wooden gods of our age.

"And she shall follow after her lovers, but she shall not overtake them ... then shall she say, "I will go and return to my first husband; for then was it better with me than now!" (Hosea 2:7).

CHAPTER TWO: JOEL, OBADIAH AND JONAH – THE LOCUST YEARS

In this chapter we will look at some of the shorter books. Joel is only three chapters long, Obadiah only one. Historically they have many things in common. There is no clear indication of the date of either but what inferences there are to be drawn point to much the same period in history. In Joel chapter three, a number of enemies are mentioned who also appear in the story of Jehoram's terrible reign, in 2 Chronicles chapter 21. If the relationship is accepted, the date of Joel would be earlier than the other Minor Prophets, as early as 800 B.C. The only evidence to date Obadiah is the references in verses 11 to 14 that may be to historical events in the time of Jehoram or Ahaz, although they could equally apply to the much later time of Jeremiah.

Joel

Joel was the son of Pethuel, and that is all that we know about him for certain. He appears to have been a native of Judah and to have prophesied in Jerusalem. His style of speaking is very different from Hosea or Amos. There is less emotion in his voice, his figures of speech do not have such deep feeling, but a new quality is present. There is a tremendous energy that tumbles phrase upon phrase. His phrases present sharp, distinct pictures that replace each other rapidly, like images on a film:

> "Gather the people, sanctify the congregation, assemble the old men, gather the children, and those that suck the breasts; let the bridegroom go forth of his chamber, and the bride out of her closet" (Joel 2:16).

The first part of Joel is concerned with a series of agricultural plagues that were causing famine. "That which the palmerworm hath left hath the locust eaten; and that which the locust hath left hath the cankerworm eaten ..." (Joel 1:4). There was a series of such plagues in Palestine such as had never been remembered before. Joel recognised them as the direct action of God, the warning of the approaching day of the LORD. If the early date for Joel is correct, this would be the first use of this term that is frequently applied later to describe God's intervention in history. It does not refer to one specific event, but to a time when God steps into action, and carries with it overtones of judgement, of the end of a phase of human carelessness and disobedience. The prophets live in an age of corruption because of sin, God had promised an age of fulfilment, of wholeness and righteousness, and the cataclysmic period that would work the change is the day of the LORD. In the letters of Peter and Paul, the term is used for the coming of Christ in judgement and the period following it.

It is surprising to find how much the three chapters of Joel have supplied us with well-known phrases and quotations that we often see but rarely credit to source. The writers of the New Testament echo his words, particularly in passages describing future events. Joel 2:28-32 was quoted by Peter on the day of Pentecost, and we have the impression that he must have known the book almost by heart. John, in the Revelation, describes a plague of locusts very similarly to the way Joel presented his picture. In chapter three we discover the words that have become a challenge to evangelical Christianity, "Multitudes, multitudes in the valley of decision! For the day of the LORD is near in the valley of decision". The verse is often taken out of context, because the valley Joel speaks about is the valley of Jehoshaphat and the decision is in the hands of God, "For there will I sit to judge all the nations round about"; but the words are a challenge to our complacency.

There is almost always, in the prophets, a statement of all-conquering love that will eventually triumph over the deadly selfishness of men. "Rend your heart, and not your garments, and turn unto the LORD your God: for He is gracious and full of compassion, slow to anger, and plenteous in mercy." It is this God who promises to restore unto them the years that the locust has eaten. That is a wonderful phrase and a wonderful promise. There are years in our own lives that the locusts took but, thank God, the promise stands that He will restore the things that He did not take away.

Obadiah

Obadiah is a very short prophecy directed specifically against Edom. We know nothing more about the prophet than his name. The remarkable thing about the book is that it made specific promises about a proud nation and that they are proven true in the geography of our time.

"The pride of thine heart hath deceived thee, O Thou that dwellest in the clefts of the rock, whose habitation is high, that saith in his heart, who shall bring me down to the ground?" (v.3).

This description of Petra, the city of wonder at the heart of the caravan routes, is graphic, but the fate of Petra was sad. "The men that were at peace with thee have destroyed thee" (v.7). The city is described by H. V. Morton. "We went on over a stony track with tall cliffs on each side; honeycombed with black entrances to tombs, houses and temples". Morton adds, "If I had to select one place among all the places I know in the world where the spirit of desolation might have its home, I would choose the dead city of Petra". The mountains around the city are crowned with the high places of forgotten local deities.

In the 5th century B.C. the Nabataeans, a trading people, took over Petra. They swallowed up the civilisation of Edom and most of what remains is their work. Aretas, father-in-law of Herod Antipas and ruler of Damascus at the time of Paul's escape, was a member of this nation. The city was captured by Trajan in 106 A.D. and lay desolate for years. In the 7th century the Moslem invaders destroyed it again. In the 12th century the Crusaders built a fort there. After that it was forgotten until, in 1812, Burckhardt rediscovered its existence. It stands as a witness to the fact that God will always keep His word.

Jonah

Finally, we come to the four chapters of Jonah. His story is so well known that we do not need to repeat it and will keep off the well-worn paths. The book is more easily placed because there is a reference to the prophet, who foretold the territorial expansion that would take place in the reign of Jeroboam II (2 Kings 14:25). This would make Jonah roughly contemporary with Amos and it casts light upon the state of the rising nation of Assyria. Jonah came from Gath-hepher in Zebulun, a few miles north of Nazareth. From this little place he went to a great city whose magnificence is increased by every fresh discovery of the archaeologists.

The lesson of Jonah is the lesson of responsibility. When God sends a man into a position of danger, it is because God is responsible for all the people in the world. In his selfish national pride Jonah had written Nineveh off, but God cared.

The mounds of ruins on the east bank of the Tigris mark the site of Nineveh. The palaces of Sennacherib and Esarhaddon, the library of Ashurbanipal, the royal stables and warehouses, the blocks of government buildings surrounded by wide parks and game preserves, they are all gone. Assyria came to be a hated word, the synonym for unrivalled cruelty. In the early days of the empire, there was a temporary change of heart.

The savage, hook-nosed soldiers who tore Judah apart, who raped and tortured on a searing path across the terrified nations, were the children of men who listened to Jonah. Perhaps the victims who writhed, impaled on stakes, may have denounced the God who forgave Nineveh and preserved the monster. They could also have thought that He was the same God who had forgiven them, His children, times beyond number, and that the monster lived inside themselves as well as outside. Nobody has a monopoly in God's mercy and nobody can ignore the significance of sin in his own experience.

Jonah's reason for not going to Nineveh is usually interpreted as fear, but he gives his reason in chapter 4:2. He could not bear to look foolish. He could not spend all that effort unless God would promise to act in judgement. Like Elijah, he was faced with the fact that he was less than his message. His dignity was touched, the great "I" was levelled. Elijah said, "I am not better than my fathers". In the wake of deflation came despondency and a death-wish, a denial of purpose or value. There is no escape from the despair of worthlessness except to live with the idea every day that we are expendable, "not I but Christ". Then the circumstances in which we confront the idea will not suddenly throw us off balance.

CHAPTER THREE: AMOS – THE MAN FROM TEKOA

Amos is an outstanding example of the ordinary men, mentioned in the introduction to this book, who performed extraordinary tasks. He came from Tekoa, a village about twelve miles south of Jerusalem, where he had a sheep herd that grazed in the scant pasture. He was also involved in the business of growing Sycamore fruit. It has been suggested that the journeys into the Northern Kingdom may have begun with selling wool. The thing which is clear is that he came from no school of prophets and had no prophetic vocation until God called him to deliver a series of messages in Bethel, the centre of Israelite worship. His preaching seems to have been compressed into a short space of time and to have brought him into frontal conflict with the religious authorities. We can speculate about what happened to him after he defied a deportation order, but there is no evidence. We have only a few short prophecies after the clash and then silence.

Amos prophesied in the middle of the eight century B.C. Jeroboam II came to the throne of Israel about 782 B.C. There was great prosperity and political success. In the phase between the decline of Syria and the rise of Assyria, the kingdom of Israel was restored to many of the ancient boundaries that had not been possessed since the days of David and Solomon (2 Kings 14:25). It was an era of expanding trade. Rich men had large estates, often obtained at the expense of the dispossessed poor, who were sold into slavery. Men lived in luxury on great fortunes and moved from winter to summer palaces, taking their ease and enjoying economic security. In 745 B.C., Tiglath Pileser came to the throne of Assyria and the days of Israel were numbered. God had numbered them long before. The people had chosen to follow local cults or had modified the worship of Jehovah to their own whims to free themselves for personal lust or social piracy.

Amos prophesied before the earthquake and he told them that it was coming. We know little more of this event than he tells us, except that there is one further reference to it in Zechariah 14:5, but it was obviously a terrible and long-remembered catastrophe. It is striking that Amos described his message as "the words ... which he saw". The revelation of God was an experience that was imprinted upon the visual memory.

The message begins "the LORD shall roar from Zion". The initial statement denied the place of Bethel in God's plan and made clear that there was one place where God made His will known. The point to remember is that these words were spoken at the heart of a religious system that was in rivalry with Jerusalem, to a people who resented the position of Judah, by a man from the south. We can imagine Amos delivering the prophecy of the early chapters to the crowds who gathered around him in the city. After the initial statement, they would find reason to applaud. He preached doom on Damascus, on Gaza, and Tyre, on Edom, the Ammonites and Moab. Except for the lucrative trading relationships, there was little love for these nations in Israel. Then Amos turned to Judah, and again the attack would be popular with his audience, but he did not stop there. He turned on them, "For three transgressions of Israel, yea, for four, I will not turn away the punishment thereof" (Amos 2:6).

We can listen happily to denunciation of other people, we can enjoy taking our friends and enemies to pieces, but as soon as the spotlight turns upon ourselves and the voice begins to speak about our own desperate faults, we cry out in anger and all our defence systems begin to operate. Amaziah, the priest of Bethel, heard Amos out over the nations, heard the denunciation of social evil, heard the warnings of national disaster, but the day that the prophet said that "the sanctuaries of Israel shall be laid waste" (Amos 7:9) was the day that Amaziah decided that he had heard enough.

It is not possible to break through the moral laws of God without suffering the consequences. Israel was involved with a false religion, which had appearance but not reality. They had adapted God's plan to their convenience and the exigencies of the time. They were committed to the preservation of an ever higher standard of living that made their own needs a priority and placed others beyond their caring. The women, described by Amos in that unflattering term "cows of Bashan" drove their menfolk on in the search for material prosperity at all costs. The result was disaster. If there is a message in Amos for a man of the western world in the twentieth century, it must be this above anything, "woe to them that are at ease in Zion" (Amos 6:1).

God sent them warnings. Once again it is made clear that calamities and hardships in life are often the hand of God to mould and shape our way of living. There was earthquake, locusts and drought in their experience and the result was that they ran further away from God in a desperate search for other solutions. The people were told that they must seek God and live. They must not seek Him in the false places, in the religious institutions that men had created. The altars of Bethel did not hold any hope for the searchers. God had given His way to men and there was only one way. Efforts to reach security outside of that may seem successful, but the foundation is always suspect and will collapse.

It would have been much more comfortable for Amos to remain silent. It is easier to disregard moral evil than to withstand it. "He that is prudent shall keep silence in such a time" (Amos 5:13). But God does not keep silence and His prophet is bound to speak out at the cost of personal popularity and safety. He attacked their cherished beliefs. They believed that, one day, God would intervene. It was a great day ahead, but the prophet warned them that it would be an unpleasant surprise. They believed that they had a special position in God's favour, but Amos mocked their complacency. "Are ye not as the children of the Ethiopians unto Me, O children of Israel? ... Have not I brought up Israel out of the land of Egypt, and the Philistines from Caphtor, and the Syrians from Kir?" (Amos 9:7).

It was a strange position for a prophet from Judea. God chooses men by standards that are His own, and does not use human measurement. No guidance counsellor would have picked Amos for this assignment. There is still a power of guidance and divine selection at work in the world, but we can be alarmingly deaf to His voice. We can be very logical. It is impossible that a sheepherder from Judah would be asked to prophesy about the fate of Bethel. Our reasoning sounds much safer than God's because there is often too much adventure, too much faith needed for the staid, stuffy disciples to risk God's way. In any case, Amos was expended. If we are primarily interested in conserving the things that belong to us, we cannot dare to answer God's call. In God's way, a servant is expendable, as His own Son was expendable in the battle for the world that He loves.

Amaziah the priest ordered Amos to leave Israel and to confine his activities to Judah. There were many questions that Amos could not answer but on one point he was absolutely clear, that his experience of God was reality and that his reality was more important than all the arguments and threats of the men who were defending their institutions. "Thus saith the LORD", was a message that could not be silenced.

If only they had heard. If only they had shared the impracticable unreasonableness of Amos, and the reality of God's voice, there would have been a different story to tell. The little man with the lonely voice disappeared from the streets of Bethel, the memory faded in the temples and palaces, and the famine came, "not a famine of bread, nor a thirst for water, but of hearing the words of the LORD".

Amos was not wasted. God did not, even in all that, leave a desolation. His great love could not be denied and Amos closed with a promise. "I will not utterly destroy ... saith the LORD ... I will bring again the captivity of My people Israel" (Amos 9:8,14).

We are watching it with our own eyes. The message that fell upon deaf ears is now part of the history of our world and a fact in our newspapers. The word of God is the force that drives through centuries and kingdoms into our own experience so that we may deny the cold, hard voice of earthly wisdom and live in the truth of His purposes.

CHAPTER FOUR: MICAH THE MORASHTITE

Micah specified his own chronological location, in the reigns of Jotham, Ahaz and Hezekiah. These three kings reigned for a total of fifty-eight years. Jeremiah gave a specific indication when he spoke of the prophet being active in the reign of Hezekiah. Most of the prophecies in the book seem to relate to the Assyrian invasions of 711 B.C. and 701 B.C. Micah was a border dweller, citizen of a small town in the foothills at the edge of the Philistine plains, and he was a contemporary of Isaiah. A man of the country, like Amos, he saw through the tinsel covering of city society. His message spoke of the enemy inside as well as the enemy outside.

It is a startling fact that the defeats of Israel came from the enemy inside. It is fair warning to a people today that wishes to avoid defeat and would like to know more about victory. The real defeats come from inside. The enemies outside capitalised on a situation that already existed, from the defeat at Ai to the fall of Samaria. Now it was time for Micah to warn that the fate of Samaria threatened Jerusalem, "for the transgressions of Israel were found in thee." Micah met the same hard defensiveness that had greeted others, based on self-satisfaction and righteous assurance. Nothing is more rock hard than a self-righteous man. "Is not the LORD among us? No evil shall come upon us." There was no possible penetration of that armour in which the priests and the prophets strutted, and with which they inspired the population to put their trust in a tottering structure; no possible penetration except the word of the LORD.

Behind the security and affluence there was rottenness and a great vacuum, such as Amos had seen in Israel. The small farmers were being exploited by great landowners. "They covet fields, and seize them."

There was no justice in the land, that priests and the prophets were grabbing for money, and there was idolatry. Micah came to attack the system with a variety of weapons. It is good to know that, for once in a long time, the people heard the message and obeyed it, and the result was a stay of execution by the miracles of deliverance (Jeremiah 26:18,19).

One of Micah's weapons was satire. He used it sharply and with bitter skill. The last six verses of chapter one are a sequence of word plays on the names of places, like saying that, "At the Cape of Good Hope we learned to despair."

The political situation at the time was very precarious. As the Assyrian threat grew, the people of Judah had to choose. Public opinion polarised around two positions, pro-Assyrian or pro-Egyptian. Lachish was the headquarters of a new chariot brigade, obtained at great cost and highly publicised as a valuable weapon. It was a situation of choice that recurred throughout their history, the selection of a power alliance. Only a few of God's people looked upwards, when everyone else was looking north or south. It was hard in those times to remember that God had set His Name on a certain small place and that He had promised, "Happy art thou, O Israel: Who is like unto thee, a people saved by the LORD" (Deuteronomy 33.29).

It was easy to forget or to live in doubt that they were the people who had carried all before them and spread terror among nations that awaited their coming. It was easy to believe that victory in God's strength belonged in history and that nothing quite like it would ever happen again. The men who spoke in the Name of the Lord did not say that the great days were finished. There is no reason now to say that the great days are finished unless we mean that the people are not willing to abandon materialism and comfort to obey the word of the Lord.

Anything was offered to God, except the things that He asked. Every effort was made to buy His favour or to avert His displeasure except the effort that God wanted. "Wherewith shall I come before the LORD, and bow myself before the high God? Shall I come before Him with burnt offerings, with calves of a year old? Will the LORD be pleased with thousands of rams, or with ten thousands of rivers of oil? Shall I give my firstborn for my transgression, the fruit of my body for the sin of my soul?"

"Yes", they would have answered. The smoke on the altars and the ritual processions were what made them feel secure, but Micah went on, "He hath shewed thee, O man, what is good; and what doth the LORD require of thee, but to do justly, and to love mercy, and to walk humbly with thy God?"

The history of man's relationship to God, from the time of Cain, is full of instances of people who want to give Him something other than what He wants from them. The pagan concept of gods was that they were grotesque projections of human personality who had to be bribed, flattered or placated. Those who knew the God of heaven, learned that He required from men those things that were necessary for their own good, because they were necessary to life both individual and social.

Ignorance or disobedience brought people into the area of judgement, and Micah preached the inevitability of judgement. He also preached the glory of God's mercy: "He will bring me forth to the light, and I shall behold His righteousness."

CHAPTER FIVE: NAHUM, HABBAKUK AND ZEPHANIAH – THREE VOICES BEFORE DISASTER

The Voice Against Nineveh

Nahum's prophecy is very short and specific. It is easy to put a date to it because it refers back to the sack of Thebes and looks forward to the sack of Nineveh. Thebes fell in 661 B.C. The fortunes of Egypt had waxed and waned for many years, and power had shifted from city to city, from one dynasty to another. The Nubian empire was the last period of grandeur and the centre of power was the capital of the Upper Kingdom, famous for its temples of Amon. Egypt was rich in copper mines, but the rise of Assyria was coincidental with the growing use of a new metal, the coming of the Iron Age. Iron weapons were superior to bronze and there was little iron in Egypt. After long years of intermittent warfare, the armies of Ashur-bani-pal entered Egypt in 663 B.C., and in 661 B.C. the city of Thebes was sacked.

The fall of Nineveh, at the hands of an army of Medes and Babylonians, occurred in 612 B.C. All the horrors of Assyrian conquest were returned upon the heads of the people who had perpetrated them. Nahum describes graphically the terrible results of defeat to the inhabitants of a captured city.

Assyrian capitals, like those of Egypt, changed from king to king. Sargon, the destroyer of Samaria, lived at Chorsabad. Ashur-bani-pal and Sennacherib lived at Nineveh. In the British Museum it is possible to see the gigantic bulls of stone that flanked the royal gates. The great gods of Babylon, Marduk and Ashur, were physically dragged across hundreds of miles to stand in the proud city.

"Woe to the bloody city! it is all full of lies and rapine; the prey departeth not" (Nahum 3:1).

The prophecy is a solemn warning to those who make an adversary of God, but also a promise to those who put their trust in Him. It stresses the patience and longsuffering with which God deals with people, the patience expressed to Jonah, "and should not I have pity on Nineveh?"

Into the life of a nation, or an individual, God puts crises of choice, and the choice lies between obedience and friendship or disobedience and enmity. Nineveh was God's instrument of vengeance, just as Babylon later became, but the nation made the choice to become God's adversary. Opportunities for repentance and a change of course that might have changed history were refused. The refusal brought them into God's wrath and "He will make a full end of the place thereof and will pursue His enemies into darkness" (Nahum 1:8).

Nahum demonstrates a sensitive understanding of the movement of God among the nations. His message is not an angry cry for vengeance but an inspired statement of divine presence in history. The God he speaks for is the God that keeps promises, the same God who "is slow to anger" that Moses knew, but who "will by no means clear the guilty."

Habakkuk

Habakkuk grew up in good times for Judah, in the years when Nahum was prophesying, in the days of Josiah's reforms. Later Josiah tried to thwart the Pharaoh, Neccho, and died in battle at Megiddo, and evil days came with his son. Political and social perversion brought disaster that was emphasised by the contrast with better days. Nobody can rest upon past achievements. Each day, with God, is a fresh day. The old glories were no help in a day when men had turned away to idols and the Chaldean invaders were marching "through the breadth of the earth, to possess dwelling places that are not theirs".

Habakkuk wrote some time between the surrender of Jerusalem in 596 B.C. and the sack of the Temple in 586 B.C. Things were in a desperate condition in Judah and, instead of turning the nation to God, it had split and divided, both socially and politically and people were largely concerned in saving their own skins by whatever compromise or device they could make.

Habakkuk is a very beautiful book to read. There are statements about God's nature and on His dealing with people that are so profound and essential that we often quote them without realising that they come from an obscure prophet whose birthplace is not known, who wrote very little, and is not named by any other writer. The battle cry of the Reformation, the theme of Paul's letter to the Romans, is a quotation from Habakkuk, "but the just shall live by his faith" (Habakkuk 2:4).

The great vision of an earth "filled with the knowledge of the glory of the LORD, as the waters cover the sea," comes from Habakkuk 2:14. If this little book does not attract you to read or re-read any other prophet, at least read this one. He finishes with a wonderful sung prayer that speaks of the prophet's vision of God and his response to it: "When I heard, my belly trembled; My lips quivered at the voice: Rottenness entered into my bones, and I trembled in myself, That I might rest in the day of trouble." (Habbakuk 3:16 King James Version).

Through his experience, Habakkuk learned to wait quietly, despite tragedy, in the security of the knowledge that, no matter what happened, God, the LORD, would be his strength and would lift him up. The shield of faith quenches all the fiery darts for Habakkuk. Nothing can touch him because he knows, in the middle of chaos and defeat, that the light has not gone out and that disaster cannot reach God. "But the LORD is in His holy temple: Let all the earth keep silence before Him".

That is the knowledge that a man needs today, a knowledge that will preserve his integrity when it seems so necessary to come to terms and make compromise with a social system that confuses and demands so much. It was the knowledge that, a few years after this prophecy, preserved the integrity of Daniel and his friends when it would have been so easy to give up altogether.

Everything is changing. Nothing that our fathers knew, or that we learned as children, appears to be particularly relevant in the world that is falling to pieces around us; yet we are living in an unchanging reality. The reality is God, the God who has intervened in our lives in the person of Jesus Christ. This faith will preserve us from the ruin of life, whatever happens, and from the fate of Jehoiakim.

Zephaniah

This book was written, probably, just prior to the great reforms of Josiah, before 621 B.C. About this time in history the Scythian armies invaded western Asia and may be referred to in some of the passages, although not by name.

Zephaniah saw the same evils that the other prophets had seen, but he made no gentle plea for reform and repentance. The fate of Judah was decided, as God had said, "I will remove Judah also out of My sight, as I have removed Israel" (2 Kings 23,27). Zephaniah's message was one of judgement, of the approaching intervention of God in the story of Judah and her neighbours, and the end of an epoch. In the eighteenth year of Josiah the housecleaning began. There is an old Russian proverb that says, "Do not blame the mirror if your face is cracked," and Josiah looked into the mirror of God's word and saw the cracks in the nation: "Because thine heart was tender, and thou hast humbled thyself before the LORD ... I also have heard thee, saith the LORD" (2 Kings 22:19).

The story of the Minor Prophets should bring us great hope. The word of God is a powerful force and has been demonstrably so in history. Hezekiah listened to Isaiah and Micah. Nineveh listened to Jonah. Josiah heard Jeremiah and Zephaniah. The result, in each case, was a period of blessing and security for the repentant people. Zephaniah prophesied about the effect of God's intervention, His word is forthright and foretells wrath and judgement. All through the messages that roll up like black clouds, there are tiny glimpses of the sun, and suddenly, in the last chapter, the sun breaks out.

The full meaning of that final chapter will not be realised until God's purposes in human history have been accomplished. It has not happened yet but carries all the authority and hope of the ultimate phrase, "saith the LORD". It has been a long time, from man's standpoint, since Zephaniah spoke his message. The people he spoke to saw disaster, and their children have seen disaster. It would be natural for human weakness to give up on the promise and to fear that defeat and failure were to be the end of the story, except that God has spoken and His world will be fulfilled.

"Therefore wait ye for Me, saith the LORD, until the day that I rise up to the prey" (Zephaniah 3.8).

We are very conscious that God is working out His purposes in our century. The whole Middle East, which once lay dormant, has come to violent life. All the developments are part of the picture that the prophets gave us. The role of the people who put their trust in Him is to wait.

CHAPTER SIX: HAGGAI – THE PROPHET OF THE UNFINISHED HOUSE

The word of the LORD came to Haggai in 520 B.C., two years after the defeat of Gomates, the usurper, and the reinstatement of Darius Hystapes. It was addressed to the two men who held office in Jerusalem under the policy of self-government that Cyrus had initiated. The message was short, addressed specifically to the leaders, and set the model for the messages that followed. There is no indication in Scripture that Haggai was a member of the priestly family although there is an ancient tradition to this effect. Haggai's major concern was to stir up the people to build the house of God, to give God the right place. He promised, by the word of the LORD, that if their attitude was right, then God would be with them and would shake the nations on their behalf.

Haggai is very exact about the time when he received the messages and each one is dated in the second year of Darius, in the months of September, October and November. Ezra, in his history, recorded the work and effect of the prophet. The exiles who had returned to Jerusalem were having a hard time building up security and hope, many things were going wrong, and Haggai explained the reason. The fifth and sixth chapters of Ezra provide a background to the prophecy. After the accession of Darius, Haggai and Zechariah came to urge the people to renew the work that had been neglected since the exiles had arrived from Babylon with the direct purpose of rebuilding the Temple.

The book of Ezra tells the story of the journey of a large number of exiles, under Zerubbabel and Jeshua, followed about seventy-nine years later by a second group of about fifteen hundred men with Ezra. The first group had been much bigger and there must have been more hardship and difficulty in their experience than appears in the record. The problems of moving such a mass of people, of feeding and clothing and organising supplies, of helping them to find their place in the land and keeping peace with the people who had settled there, must have been considerable. Have a look at the map and see the route they would follow and the difficulties of the journey.

The organisation necessary for survival would have absorbed time and energy and left little time for luxury and ornament. They were not warmly welcomed by the new inhabitants who had been settled in Palestine and all of life was a struggle. One of the luxuries that was out of reach, in the view of the people, was the rebuilding of the house of the LORD. "It is not ... the time for the LORD's house to be built".

Haggai's main point is that there is no luxury about God's house. It is not something that we decide to afford when other needs have been met but must have absolute priority. It seems strange to describe the eternal God, who is all powerful and all love, as jealous, but He described Himself in that way to Moses (Exodus 20:5). Jealousy has a very negative connotation in contemporary usage. It is defined as suspicion or envy, but has a very different meaning in the context of God's character. It means "watchfully tenacious of rights," and God is jealous because recognition of His rights is essential to the well-being of His creation. He makes it clear that the whole man is a man who gives God first place.

Every man who lives his life above the level of complete mental confusion must establish a system of priorities. Many areas in life lay claim on time and energy. Every choice is based on the order of importance which a man has established in his mind. Happiness and fulfilment are rare because the system of priorities is wrongElijah demanded from the widow in Zarephath the first cake, although it seemed as though starvation for herself and . her son was part of the gift. The Jews in Jerusalem must have felt the same way about demands that they spend their time and energy rebuilding the Temple, yet God tells them that there can be no prosperity because the house lies in ruins.

The fact is, of course, that the exiles did start rebuilding the Temple in those difficult early days. They expended their resources in an initial enthusiasm. They gathered material, rebuilt the altar, and laid the foundation of the building. It was not until political opposition arose that the work ceased. What happened then was that the people learned to live with the fact, with the heaps of unused material and the altar standing lonely on the mountain, and turned to their own pursuits. They changed their view of life and put the Temple back behind other concerns. When somebody got troubled at the sight of work waiting to be done for the Lord they would shake their wise heads and say, "It is not the time". We learn to live with failure, to get comfortable in its company, and there is always a reason why nothing is happening. We need renewal and to hear again the instruction, "Seek ye first the kingdom of God".

God does not experience failure. The struggling group of exiles were no threat in the political world. They were a nuisance to their neighbours but could not be accused of planning aggression or of dreaming territorial expansion. In fact, they were at the mercy of the occupying forces and owed their existence to the remarkable system of justice and law that the Persian Empire had developed. Yet God promises twice, very clearly, to shake the nations and destroy the kingdoms, and all for the glory of the despised little house that they were hesitating to build.

In response to Haggai and Zechariah, the work on the Temple recommenced. Instead of spending all their time in the fields, instead of overtime in their harvest, the people gathered at the Temple and, slowly but certainly, the work went on. They sowed less but the grain grew richer, they cultivated less but the vines yielded more. The barns were fuller and their hearts were less heavy and a nation of insecure settlers began to grow into a significant people who had to be reckoned with because they were fulfilling the role that God had given them in the day that He called Abraham.

The lesson of Haggai is not unique or fresh but it is very clear and specific, "Consider your ways. "

CHAPTER SEVEN: ZECHARIAH THE PRIEST

Nehemiah records the fact that Zechariah was a priest (Nehemiah 12:1,16). He was contemporary with Haggai, but his ministry extended over a longer period, certainly until the fourth year of Darius II, 518 B.C., and possibly after that. There is no dating given to the final passages of the prophecy. In comparison with Haggai, his prophecies are more colourful, filled with imagery and with references to the future. There are passages that speak directly of the Messiah, and others that describe, with a fair amount of detail, occurrences that will take place before and during the thousand years reign of our Lord in the glorious future of Israel.

Another characteristic of Zechariah is his acquaintance with and awareness of the heavenly messengers, the angels. "These are they whom the LORD hath sent to walk to and fro through the earth" (Zechariah 1:10).

Zechariah spoke the word of the LORD, but it is significant that, to a struggling nation, painfully being reborn in the land which God had given them, surrounded by enemies, he usually refers to "the LORD of Hosts". The weak little nation, that seemed caught up in a turmoil of internal and external politics, was protected by forces greater than ever could be imagined, and was constantly the care of God. "For he that toucheth you toucheth the apple of His eye" (Zechariah 2:8).

The promises that Israel received through this prophet were enough to quicken the pulses and lift the hearts of God's people to a point where nothing could dismay or daunt them, if they had taken and treasured them. All the promises of God are real and become part of our experience through faith. It is like the story of Martha. "I know that he shall rise again in the resurrection at the last day. Jesus said unto her, I am the resurrection, and the life: he that believeth on Me, though he die, yet shall he live: and whosoever liveth and believeth on Me shall never die.... Believest thou this?" (John 11.24-26). We are always content to believe that the promises will be fulfilled in somebody's experience, some day, but He addresses them to us, and now.

Zechariah had a series of visions. Of the first, he writes, "I saw in the night, and behold a man riding upon a red horse, and he stood among the myrtle trees that were in the bottom; and behind him there were horses, red, sorrel and white" (Zechariah 1:8). Each vision is described cryptically, with little detail, but God takes great care to explain them fully. The first three are concerned with the future greatness of Israel, represented by the small community around Jerusalem, and God reveals to His prophet that the unseen messengers surround the people to protect them.

The visions of chapters three and four involve the two leaders of the people, Joshua and Zerubbabel. There must sometimes have been doubts in their minds about the validity of their leadership. Like all leaders they must have come under attack and criticism, and have felt the cold hand of despair when things seemed to be going wrong. Zechariah's word from the LORD is an assurance of their position in God's purposes and of His choice of them. It makes a great deal of difference, when we begin to doubt our judgement and to question our standing in the mists that Satan gathers round us, to hear the voice of God, "Is not this a brand plucked out the fire?" (Zechariah 3:2).

Zechariah does not direct his words against individual sins. He calls for a general repentance and a positive commitment to God's cause.

The first vision was of the man among the myrtle trees. It was a rendezvous for the LORD'S patrols which went to and fro in the earth. After nearly seventy years of sorrowful disruption, they were able to report that the earth was at rest. The punishment had destroyed

Jerusalem and the Temple, and wrecked the state, but Zechariah was very sure that God, committed to the salvation of Israel, had returned to His city and would restore it.

The second vision was four horns that represented those forces that destroyed Israel and Judah. God promised that those nations would be cast down.

The third vision was of the man who was going to measure Jerusalem. The people in the city were insecure and uncertain because the city had no wall around it. The LORD "will be unto her a wall of fire, and I will be the glory in the midst of her" (Zechariah 2:5).

The fourth and fifth visions are those already referred to, addressed to the leaders. The message to Joshua sees him standing before the angel of the LORD, with Satan, his adversary, at his right hand. The complaint seems to be that Joshua was not fit to be there. The Lord ordered that the high priest should be clothed in suitable dress.

The fifth is the well-known vision of the lampstand and the olive trees. "Not by might, nor by power, but by My Spirit, saith the LORD of Hosts" (Zechariah 4:6). It is a vision that precedes the great New Testament revelation of the work of the Holy Spirit, and once again illustrates how God has chosen many different times and people to draw back the veil and reveal the reality of His presence and His manner of working in the world.

The sixth vision (Zechariah 5:1-4) was the flying scroll of judgement, a roll thirty feet long and fifteen feet wide, bringing a curse to thieves and to those who swear falsely in the LORD's name. The final two visions (Zechariah 5.5-11; 6.1-8) concern the removal of evil from the land, and the coming of rest to the north country, Babylonia.

After the visions came a series of practical instructions and exhortations. In chapter seven, the prophet answers questions regarding the continuation of the fast for the destruction of Jerusalem and the Temple. God's answer is that the people should listen to the words that had been spoken by earlier prophets and ignored by their fathers. To fast or not to fast was no significant question because God's concern was with the lack of love and social justice. The lesson of history to the questioners was clear, and the result of disobedience was fresh in their experience in the distant streets of Babylon.

Chapters nine to fourteen contain a series of burdens or oracles. In chapter nine there is a clear prophecy of the fate of Tyre, fulfilled by the armies of Alexander the Great. In the middle of the chapter (vv.9,10) there is a short prophecy, appearing strangely in a largely unrelated context, that became reality on the day when Christ rode the colt into Jerusalem. It illustrates the ways of prophecy, where we cannot expect to discover the laws of sequence that we are accustomed to find in contemporary writing.

These later chapters appear to have been spoken at some time much later than the first years of Darius II. The spiritual leadership of the nation had declined dramatically. Again, in the allegory of the shepherds, we suddenly meet a prophecy that was remarkably fulfilled in the treachery of Judas, the deal of the thirty pieces of silver (Zechariah 11:12,13).

In chapter 13, there is a further reference to our Lord, that is quoted in the Gospels, where the prophet speaks of the smiting of the shepherd and the scattering of the sheep (vv.7,8).

The final chapter is a picture of the day of the LORD, a phrase which had, by this time, come to have a special meaning to God's people. The description contains some amazing facts, including the specific locations of a number of incidents and the details of a geographical upheaval that will change the face of the whole Middle East.

Zechariah closes with a beautiful picture of a society where everything exists for the LORD and all nations exist for His worship; a picture of a world centred around the house of the Lord God of Israel.

CHAPTER EIGHT: MALACHI – THE END OF THE LINE

The last book of the Old Testament is a sad one. It summarizes the theme of a fossilized people who did not respond to the love and life of God. The story is told in a series of "whereins", seven questions in answer to God's statements.

Malachi must have written late, probably after the time of Ezra and Nehemiah. The evils that caused concern to them seem to have grown into fixed social behaviour that was typical of the people of Israel. He does not mention any historical events or any point of reference to fix his place in time, but there is an atmosphere of finality. The feeling is that hope lies only with the remnant within the remnant.

The most terrible "wherein" is the first (Malachi 1:2), "I have loved you, saith the LORD. Yet ye say, Wherein hast Thou loved us?" God had set His eye upon Jacob, nursed him from childhood, cared for him, rescued him from the results of his own foolishness, trained him, protected him, given and given and given. It is a hard blow to any parent when a child turns round and says, "You don't love me". In a normal parent, part of the blow and the pain is the memory of times when love for the child was less than it should have been, when selfishness or weakness caused failure. God's love for Jacob was a perfect love, one that never failed, but Jacob refused to see. When things went wrong, because of intent and actions, the people mocked God with complaints that He did not love them. We, who owe Him our lives, our past, our future, our selves, can never doubt His love. Can we?

"Yet I loved Jacob; but Esau I hated". That is a hard saying to hear. It has been interpreted as a relative term, as meaning, "Esau I loved less", but this is playing with words to try to make ourselves feel more comfortable. Reality is often uncomfortable and God's hatred is as much a reality as His wrath. It is part of the climate in which men live, perhaps always but certainly often, by choice. Esau is the example of the man who shut God out, and shut himself out from God. He chose the life which offered him what he wanted and, when he chose, he did not believe that he would have to take the environment in its entirety, that he could not pick and choose. I live in Canada because it offers some of the things I find rewarding in life. I did not come because I like four months of hard winter, ice storms and snowstorms and sub-zero temperatures, but they are part of what I have chosen. A man shut off from God, shuts himself off from love and salvation, and chooses to refuse them.

The next "wherein" comes from the priests who say, "Wherein have we despised Thy Name?" (Malachi 1:6). They had grown weary of serving God. There was no meaning left in it for them, and it had become a mechanical ritual. It is a dreadful fact that service can be carried on without purpose. They had practical reasons for continuing the service. It was the "proper" thing to do, their livelihood depended on it, it pleased the common people and was expected; but it was so unreal to them that they were giving God much less respect than they gave a governor. They were ready to cheat Him, but not human authority.

Boredom and indifference are no use in God's service. It should always be exciting, alive and meaningful. If it becomes dreary and monotonous there is something seriously wrong and God would prefer to have the doors of His house closed because it no longer serves a purpose. The failure of the priests was very serious because it brought the whole Temple service into disrepute, and rendered the testimony ineffectual. Men had lost their confidence and respect for God's work.

The fourth query (Malachi 2:17) involved the problem of sexual morality and the divorce laws. Treacherous dealings were typical of relationships in the nation. The whole structure of God's dealings with

His people was a tightly meshed plan for their well-being, and malpractice in one area affected the whole. The picture is summed up in the question, "Wherein have we wearied Him?" The moral scale, standard of right and wrong, had been turned upside down, and society was defining right as wrong and wrong as right. There was total confusion because the people had let go their hold on truth.

In the sad world of Malachi, there are two points worth remembering. It is not all darkness and despondency. It would be so easy to see the story of the Old Testament as a tale of disaster and to lose hope. It would be even simpler to see the story of our modern world as a tale without hope or meaning, "full of sound and fury, signifying nothing". Human philosophy is often represented by this view, from the earliest days of Greece, to the modern existentialists. God's word presents a different view.

The first point that Malachi makes is that God always has His remnant. "And they shall be Mine, said the LORD of hosts, in the day that I do make, even a peculiar treasure; and I will spare them, as a man spareth his own son that serveth him" (Malachi 3:17). However dark the night may get, there is one thing absolutely certain: the light will never go out. "Here is the patience of the saints, they that keep the commandments of God, and the faith of Jesus" (Revelation 14:12).

The second point that Malachi makes consistently is that when people lose their perspective about God, they cannot serve Him with meaning. The true servants are those who fear the LORD, the false servants are those who do not fear.

If the knowledge of God is a real experience to us, we will have a concept in mind which will affect all our actions. The concepts of father or mother or employer, the meanings we apply to a doctor or policeman, mould our actions and relationships. A criminal has a different concept of law than you or I, and he acts differently in relationship to it. The Eternal God, Creator and Upholder of all things, always present and always active in His universe, expects that we His servants, who live by His grace for a short time in this little earth, will respect and honour Him. He did not hide Himself, but "knowing God, they glorified Him not as God" (Romans 1:21), and men cut themselves off from the truth and exchanged it for a lie.

If we know God, we will fear Him. If we know God we will love Him and serve Him. The people in Malachi's time had lost the desire to serve because they no longer loved or feared or knew the LORD who loved them with an everlasting love. They had all the ritual but it was dead; they had all the appearances but there was no meaning. Malachi makes a man look inside himself and ask the questions that nobody else can answer for him.

CHAPTER NINE: THE PROPHETS AND THE GOSPEL

The messages of the prophets speak about single occurrences and about general trends of history, concern themselves with individuals and nations, correct specific sins and general evils. There are many direct references to coming events and statements about aspects of the gospel story, seeds of the future carried in the prophetic utterance. These are often quoted, and this final article is not designed to identify or list them because that would be a subject, sometimes a controversial subject, on its own. The concern this month is to draw from the prophets some of the things they say about God and His relationship to man that present facets of the Good News in such a way that it would be impossible to find a clearer picture anywhere.

It is as though a picture was painted, but because it stood in the semi-darkness it was not truly appreciated until, with the coming of Christ, the dawn light shone and the significance of the picture was understood. It is a mistake to ignore the contribution of the prophets. Perhaps the shallow, sentimental propaganda that sometimes passes as gospel preaching would be avoided if the whole picture was seen and appreciated.

There are, for example, no clearer and more dramatic statements about the authority and omnipotence of God than in the prophets. The word of the LORD of Hosts to Zechariah, "Thus saith the LORD which stretcheth forth the heavens, and layeth the foundation of the earth, and formeth the spirit of man within him" (Zechariah 12:1) is an assurance that God has never abandoned His absolute power over the nations of this world. The message to Joel repeats over and over the warning that, although the whole world is in rebellion, and the nations appear to have thrown off the reins of authority, God is in control.

Obadiah and Jonah both remind us that God is watching the conduct of the nations with a close care and that history tells the tale of His work.

It seems hard to believe that the world could be so mad as to rebel against God. It might seem reasonable that, in ignorance, a man or a nation would go against His wishes, but it is clear from the prophets that the blindness of rebellion is a deliberate choice and that, as human reason is deified, Almighty God is denied. Haggai shows us that sin is leaving God out.

In Isaiah 24, the prophet speaks of the time of the shaking of the foundations of the earth. "The earth is utterly broken, the earth is clean dissolved, the earth is moved exceedingly. The earth shall stagger like a drunken man, and shall be moved to and fro like a hut" (Isaiah 24:19-20). After the song of destruction, Isaiah bursts into a song of faith, "O LORD, Thou art my God" (Isaiah 25:1). There is no neutral ground in the prophets' view. The world is a battlefield where men either accept or reject the meaning of God's existence; they either give allegiance or rebel. Micah makes it very clear that God cannot be bought or moulded or changed, He must be accepted as He is. "Will the LORD be pleased with thousands of rams?"

Just as clearly as they portray the authority of God, the prophets describe the nature of sin. The self-centred life is sin, and brings destruction. Habakkuk is one of the writers who dealt with this. Opposition or deafness to God's word is sin. The consequences of sin are desolation and destruction without fail, because of judgement. It is not a question of saying that sin may bring down God's judgement, it will. Hosea illustrates how judgement is the outworking of sin. The epistle to the Romans does not say that "the wages of sin may be death". There is no "may be". Judgement is, to borrow a phrase from Campbell

Morgan, "love's passionate anger". "Woe to her that is rebellious and polluted, to the oppressing city! She obeyed not the voice; she received not correction; she trusted not in the LORD" (Zephaniah 3:1, 2).

Nahum illustrates how fearful a thing it is to fall under the judgement of God. He "will pursue His enemies into darkness". If we want to find the key to the meaning of the human story, whether it is a personal or a national history, it lies in the balance of mercy and judgement, and that balance is in God's hand.

All the prophets, then, have a great deal to say about the consequences of sin and disobedience to Almighty God. They dramatically portray the meaning of judgement and how incontrovertibly it follows after the men or the nations who disregard the claims of the Creator. If that was all they said, it would be a major contribution, but there is more.

Love has a passionate anger, but it also has a patient purpose. "The LORD thy God is in the midst of Thee, a mighty One who will save: He will rejoice over thee with joy, He will rest in His love" (Zephaniah 3:17). Time after time the message of judgement, the promise of terrible destruction, suddenly turns into a statement that, in the end, God is a God of restoration and hope. Hosea illustrates how love continues through infidelity and suffering. Judgement brings suffering to the offender, but love brings suffering to the lover: "My well-beloved had a vineyard in a very fruitful hill" Isaiah says. "What could have been done more to My vineyard that I have not done in it?" (Isaiah 5:1, 4).

The ultimate triumph of love is a part of the message of the prophets. "I will spare them, as a man spareth his own son that serveth him" (Malachi 3:17). "For the mountains shall depart, and the hills shall be removed; but My kindness shall not depart from thee, neither shall My covenant of peace be removed, saith the LORD" (Isaiah 54:10).

It is very plainly stated that, out of the chaos of destruction that accompanies sin, God is going to make a new thing. "Behold, I will do a new thing; now shall it spring forth" (Isaiah 43:19). "For the LORD hath created a new thing in the earth" (Jeremiah 31:22).

There is a great surge of humanitarian feeling in our world. Many voices are crying for a new way of relating to people, for the abandonment of prejudice and hatred. The prophets say very definitely that the only basis for proper relationships between people is a proper relationship to God.

"He hath shewed thee, O man, what is good; and what doth the LORD require of thee, but to do justly, and to love mercy, and to walk humbly with thy God?" (Micah 6:8). To "do justly" is to maintain honest relationships; to "love mercy" is to love kindness and goodwill, and to "walk humbly" is to be content and submissive. The Good News for our time is that the kind of relationships that men are crying out to enjoy are possible, when a man is living in proper relationship to God.

While the earth wears out around us and it seems that everything is going to pieces, God remains unchanged and changeless; I AM. His judgement, His mercy and love, and His expectations of men do not change.

"For the vision is yet for the appointed time, and it hasteth toward the end, and shall not lie: though it tarry, wait for it; because it will surely come, it will not delay. Behold, his soul is puffed up, it is not upright in him: but the just shall live by his faith" (Habakkuk 2:3,4).

After Malachi there was a silence, and then a voice began to cry in the wilderness, "Make ye ready the way of the Lord". God's purposes were going forward despite all that had happened and all that was happening. Our only security lies in a true and honest relationship with

Him which is available through Jesus Christ. The prophets pointed the need in which men lived, and the goal to which they must aim. The Son of God opened up the way.

CHAPTER TEN: WHAT IS A PROPHET?

How is a prophet different from a priest? Is a prophet born or made? Is he a prophet for a short while, because he is called to a task, and then he ceases to be a prophet? How is a true prophet distinguished from a false one? What is a prophet? It may seem unusual, at the end of a book on the prophets, to ask a question that might have been answered at the beginning. Perhaps, logically, it should have been asked in the opening chapter, but the reason for postponement is that the experience of meeting the men who played the role in their time may provide material for a more informed and critical answer.

The work of the prophet is usually concerned with crisis. It has its special significance in a specific period of time. The situation may not seem particularly critical to the people that receive the prophetic messages because they are not always aware of the meaning of the events that happen around them, but God's eyes see the crisis. Every time of choice is a critical time in human experience. The role of the prophet is to reveal the nature and true significance of the situation by the word of the Lord.

A priest served in a recognized framework of behaviour. There were clear guidelines inside which he worked. A prophet had no such framework and his behaviour and message were often in conflict with the conventions of his time. There were standards by which his message could be measured but the people neglected to use them.

People long to be flattered. They want glorification, approval and support. The true prophet cannot provide what they want. His message is measured against the historic word and is its living reality in the present. The people of Israel measured it by other standards and refused to hear. They tried to close the prophet's lips by persecution or murder. It was not only enemies that would threaten a prophet, his friends posed a different kind of threat. He was a lonely man.

The prophets were called by God. They were not self-appointed to their work. In a number of cases there was a vision that preceded the call. Isaiah described the stages of his summons in detail in chapter 6; there was a vision, purification, the call and the response. Jeremiah describes similar circumstances and Ezekiel also. The first fact that any prophet had to face was his own total unworthiness to handle the message that was being delivered through his lips.

We know very little about the schools of prophets that existed in the days of the early kings, or what part they played in the life of the nation, but by the time of the minor prophets the men whose messages have been preserved for us all seem to have stood on their own. No human experience or training was able to fit them for the task of their lives. It must have been a very fearsome thing for ordinary men to find themselves responsible to bring the battering ram of the word of the Lord to bear on the complacency and ignorance of the people. It is not surprising that the response would be, "I am a man of unclean lips, and I dwell in the midst of a people of unclean lips". There was no room for pride or self-satisfaction in a prophet.

It is important to clarify this point about the prophetic task. The prophet did not say, "I don't like what is going on and I will speak my mind in the name of the LORD". He did not adopt a religious or philosophical standpoint and spread propaganda to involve other people in his ideology. He was abandoned to the word of the LORD, beyond the security of his personal ideas or safety.

It is true that a great part of the message of the prophets was addressed to social issues and much has been made of this at different times by people who seemed to want to confine the gospel to social issues.

The emphasis of the prophets is strong evidence of God's involvement, and there is no doubt that God is concerned with human society. He has always been concerned with the relationships of people, whether private or social or business. The reason for the concern with such issues is that relationships with other persons are a part of spiritual crisis. We have enough information in the epistles of James and John alone to convince us that relationships and the way we deal with other people are of the greatest importance.

The sins that were attacked were many. It may be interesting to notice that the same sins were attacked by the Lord Himself when He spoke to the people. He spoke against the abuse of economic power, false leadership, blindness and narrowness of vision, and pride.

The prevailing popular idea of a prophet is that he is a seer to tell the future. Emphasis has been laid upon the ability to foretell events with accuracy and precision. While it is true that much of their message is concerned with future events, the predictions are incidental to the main purpose of the message.

God is a God of history and in the Old Testament it was largely the history of Israel, but that history is not just the story of the past, it is also the future. The future is as clearly defined by God as the past except that a great deal has to be expressed in conditional terms, because its nature is consequential. "If they speak not according to this word, it is because there is no light in them. And they shall pass through it, hardly bestead and hungry" (Isaiah 8, 20, 21 King James Version). Unfortunately for human history, the positive conditions were rarely fulfilled and the negative conditions were met frequently. It was unusual that the predictions of a message like Jonah's were not fulfilled because a nation changed its ways and sought the way of life.

When a word of prophecy is given, it must be heard and obeyed if there is to be any blessing. It does not have to be heard and obeyed because God always leaves men with a choice. The role of the prophet is to make that choice very clear and plain by rolling back the mists of prejudice and misconception and bringing in the light of God's word. He leaves people with the truth and with the responsibility for making a decision.

[1] Hos.1:2

[2] Ezek.16:32

[3] Hos.1.2

[4] Hos.1:3-9

[5] See 2 Kgs 9-10

[6] Ex.33:15

[7] Gen.12:2-3; Gen.13:15-16

[8] Hos.1:10

[9] Ezra 8:35

[10] Hos.2:14-23

[11] Isa.49:6, Rom.9:24-25

[12] Hos.3:4-5

[13] Jer.30:9, Ezek.34:24

[14] Hos.4:8

[15] Lk.12:48, Jas.3:1

[16] Hos.11:8 (17) (18)

[17] Jer.31:3

[18] Hos.3:1-3

[19] 2 Tim.2:13, Isa.14:24

[20] 1 Chron.9:3

[21] 2 Chron.30:11,18

[22] Rev.5:5

[23] Hos.14:1

[24] Hos.14:4,8

[25] Hos.3:3

[26] Rom.8:32

[27] Matt.12:7, quoting Hos.6:6

[28] Hos.2:5

[29] Hos.6:4

[30] Jer.31:3

[31] Hos.3:2

[32] Hos.14:1

[33] Hos.1:11

[34] 1 Pet.2:10

[35] Hos.11:3-4

[36] Hos.11:8

[37] Rom.9:25-26

[38] 2 Chron.26:5 NIV

[39] 2 Chron.26:22

[40] 2 Chron.27:6 RV

[41] v.2 NIV

[42] Hos.1:4 NIV

[43] 1 Cor.4:15; 1 Cor.7:8

[44] Ps.68:6 NIV

[45] Prov.20:4

[46] Hos.1:11

[47] Hos.1:6

[48] Hos.1:9

[49] Acts 4:32

[50] Acts 4:24 RV

[51] Hos.1:10

[52] Hos.2:1

[53] Ps.73:28

[54] Lk.8:14 RV

[55] Hos.14:1-2

[56] Songs 2:14

[57] 1 Pet.1:18

[58] Songs 8:13

[59] Joel 1:15; Joel 2:1,11,31; Joel 3:14

[60] Joel 1:15; Joel 2:1

[61] Joel 3:1

[62] Joel 2:28

[63] Joel 2:31; see also Joel 3:15

[64] Joel 3:14

[65] Mal.4:5

[66] 2 Thess.2:3

[67] Jn 2:18

[68] Rev.13

[69] 2 Thess.2:3-4

[70] Matt.24:29-30

[71] Matt.24:21 & 29

[72] Note that this does not appear to be the 'final' instalment of the day of the Lord. 2 Pet.3:10 supplies new information which cannot be ascertained from the Old Testament prophecies concerning the day of the Lord. He points to a final instalment of the day of the Lord at the close of the millennium and prior to our entering the eternal age, the day of God.

[73] Rev.19:15-16

[74] Joel 1:15

[75] 1 Thess.5:4

[76] 1 Thess.5:11

[77] Joel 2:26-27

[78] 1 Thess.5:9

[79] 2 Thess.2:2

[80] Joel 1:5

[81] Joel 1:13

[82] Joel 2:12

[83] 1 Thess.5:6

[84] 1 Thess.5:2-3

[85] Joel 2:1

[86] Lk.13:4

[87] Jn.9:1-3

[88] Gen.3

[89] Rom.8:32

[90] Amos 7:14-15

[91] Amos 1:1; see 2 Chron.11:1-6

[92] See 1 Kgs12.16-33 for Jeroboam I, 2 Kgs.14.23-29 for Jeroboam II and 2 Chron.26 for Uzziah

[93] 2 Kgs.14:25

[94] Isa.6:1

[95] Amos 1:3

[96] 2 Kgs.10:32-33

[97] 2 Kgs.14:26

[98] Amos 1:5

[99] 2 Kgs.14:28

[100] 2 Kgs.16:9 - they also exiled the Northern kingdom, Israel, from their land (2 Kgs.17:6)

[101] Amos 1:3,6,9,11,13; Amos 2:1

[102] Amos 2:4-5

[103] 2 Kgs.25:9

[104] Amos 2:6-7

[105] Ex.22:26

[106] Amos 4:6,8,9,10,11

[107] Heb.12:5-6

[108] Acts 7:42-43 Stephen quoting the Gk Old Testament from memory, with variations from the Hebrew

[109] Amos 5:18

[110] Rev.3:14-27

[111] Gen.28:10-22

[112] See Deut.12:1-14; 1 Kgs.9:3

[113] 1 Kgs.12:29

[114] Amos 3:14; 4:4; Amos 5:5-6

[115] Amos 8:5

[116] Amos 9:11-12

[117] Acts 15:14

[118] Amos 9:15

[119] Amos 2:6-8; 4:1; 5:11-12.

[120] Amos 5:11

[121] Amos 6:4-6

[122] Leviticus 19:9-10,15; Deuteronomy 15:7-11; 24:14-15, 17-22

[123] Amos 5:21-23

[124] Jas.2:1-9

[125] Jas.5:1-6

[126] 1 Cor.1:26-28

[127] 2 Cor.2:14-15

[128] Burgon, J., William Petra

[129] Obad. vv3-4

[130] Obad. v.8

[131] Kipling, R., Recessional

[132] 1 Cor.1:19-24

[133] Prov.16:18

[134] 2 Kgs. 14:25,26

[135] Jonah 1:1,2

[136] Gen.10:8-12

[137] 2 Kgs. 14:25

[138] Jonah 1:2

[139] Jonah 3:3

[140] Jonah 4:11

[141] Acts 10:34b-35

[142] Jonah 4:1

[143] Jonah 4:3

[144] Jonah 4:4

[145] Jer.12:14-16

[146] Lam.3:31-33

[147] Col.2:9

[148] Matt.9:36-38

[149] Matt.15:32

[150] Mk.1:40-41

[151] 1 Pet.3:8-9

[152] Jonah 2:9

[153] Jonah 1:2

[154] Ezek.18:23,32

[155] Gen.18:20-23

[156] Jonah 2:8

[157] Jonah 4:1

[158] Jonah 4:5-11

[159] Matt.28:18-20

[160] Mic.3:1-3

[161] Mic.3:5-6

[162] Mic.3:9-12

[163] Mal.2:7

[164] Mic.5:1-7

[165] Acts 3:14-15 NSB

[166] Acts 5:30-32 NASB

[167] Jn.14:6

[168] Heb.12:1-2

[169] Mic.5:4-5

[170] Ex.14:30

[171] Num.13:23-24

[172] Deut.1:27-28

[173] Heb.3:18-19

[174] Deut.28:1,2,40

[175] Ps.84:2

[176] Ps.19:10

[177] Is.26:9 RV margin

[178] 1 Pet.2:2

[179] Ex.23:20

[180] Mic.5:2

[181] Mk.11-13

[182] Mic.7:1

[183] Mal.3:10

[184] Nah.1:2

[185] Nah.1:3

[186] Nah.1:7-9

[187] Nah.1:11

[188] Jon.3:5-10

[189] Rom.6:1

[190] Nah.1:14

[191] Nah.3:3,10

[192] Gal.6:7

[193] Rom.14:12

[194] Nah.3:16

[195] Nah.3:1

[196] Nah.3:19

[197] Hab.1:2-4

[198] 609-598 BC Jer.22:11-19

[199] 612 BC See Neh.2&3; Zeph.2:13-15

[200] Jer.50:23

[201] Hab.1:5-11

[202] e.g. 'Another day, yet another terror attack' (Daily Mail (UK) front page headline 23 July 2016)

[203] Hab.1:12-13 cf Deut.32:4,15; Ps.5:4-5

[204] "We will not die" Hab.1:12

[205] Hab.1:2

[206] Hab.1:13

[207] Hab.1:17

[208] Job 7:17-21

[209] Rev.6:9-10

[210] Hab.1:12

[211] Hab.1:5

[212] Jer.5:12

[213] Hab.1:1

[214] Hab.2:2

[215] Hab.2:20

[216] Hab.2:13

[217] Eph.1:10

[218] Hab.2:14

[219] Isa.11:9

[220] Rev.1:7

[221] Gal.6:7 (26)

[222] Hab.2:4-20

[223] Rev.20:11-15

[224] Hab.2:4

[225] See vv.2 & 16

[226] v.3-15

[227] 539BC

[228] 2 Thess.1:9

[229] Heb.13:5

[230] v.18

[231] 1 Cor.15:25; Ps.2:8-9

[232] Hab.1:2-4

[233] Hab.1:13

[234] Hab.2:4

[235] Rom.1:17

[236] Hab.2:5-16

[237] Hab.3:6-16

[238] Hab.3:17-18

[239] Mic.3:11

[240] Mic.7:3

[241] Mic.7:6

[242] Mich.2:3

[243] Mic.7:18-19

[244] Mic.5:4; 7:14

[245] Mic.7:7

[246] Mic.5:2

[247] Mic.5:4

[248] Mic.6:8

[249] 2 Thess.2:3ff

[250] Zeph.1:14-15

[251] 2 Chron:29.11

[252] Rev.3:16

[253] Zeph.3:12-13

[254] 2 Cor.5:11

[255] 2 Cor.5:14

[256] Matt.6:21

[257] Hag.1:5,7

[258] 1 Cor.3:9

[259] 1 Cor.3:16

[260] Eph.2:21, RV

[261] Hag.1:2

[262] Hag.2:3

[263] Hag.1:8

[264] Matt.28:19

[265] Jn 4:35

[266] 2 Cor.6:2

[267] Hag.1:4

[268] Ex.20:3, RV margin

[269] Hag.1:6

[270] Hag.1:12

[271] Matt.6:33

[272] Matt.6:28, RV

[273] Hag.1:4

[274] Hag.1:8

[275] Lk.2:49 ESV

[276] Hag.2:4

[277] Hag.2:19

[278] Zech.4:10NIV

[279] Ezra 5:1

[280] Zech.1:16

[281] Zech.1:17; Zech.2:12; Zech.3:2

[282] Zech.8:8; cf Deut.7:6-8; Ezek.36:22-23

[283] Zech.8:2 NIV

[284] Zech.8:11

[285] Zech.7:8-10; Zech.8:16-17

[286] Zech.8:23. Cf. Isa.2:2-4; Mic.4:1-5

[287] Ps.2:6-8

[288] Zech.2:4-5; Zech.14:10-11,16-21; Zech.2:5; Zech.3:10

[289] Zech.4:6-10; Zech.3:4-7

[290] Gal.3:5; Rev.1:12-20

[291] Isa.6:1; Heb.2:9

[292] Zech.3:8; Jer.23:5; Jer.33:15-16

[293] Zech.6:12-13

[294] Zech.10:2-3; Zech.11:15-17; cf. Ezek.34:1-10

[295] Zech.10:3-8

[296] Zech.11:12-13. The Hebrew word for 'potter' sounds like that for 'treasury'. In Matt.27:3-9 the Spirit takes and uses both words.

[297] Zech.13:7; Isa.53:10

[298] Zech.9:9; Matt.21:4-5; Jn 12:14-15

[299] Zech.2:10-11; Zech.12:10

[300] Zech.9:10

[301] Ezra 5:1,2

[302] Hag.1:8; 1 Cor.3:9-17

[303] Zech.4:2-3

[304] Heb.1.3

[305] Lev.24:2

[306] Rev.1:10-20

[307] Jn.8:12

[308] Matt.5:15-16

[309] Eccl.3:7

[310] Mal.1:1

[311] Mal.3:1

[312] Mal.3:2-3

[313] Mal.1:1

[314] Mal.1:2

[315] Eph.1:4

[316] 2 Tim.2:12-13

[317] Mal.1:6

[318] p.77, NT 1948

[319] Mal.2:2

[320] Mal.2:17

[321] Mal.4:2

[322] Mal.3:17

[323] Mal.4:2

[324] Mal.3:1

[325] Is.53:5; 1 Pet.2:24

[326] Mal.3:7

[327] Is.53:3

[328] Rom.11:15

[329] Mal.3:10

[330] Blanchard, J., "Major Points from the Minor Prophets", E.P. Books 2012, p. 255)

[331] Acts 20:24

[332] 1 Jn.2:28-29

[333] Mal.4:2

[334] 2 Pet.3:3-4

[335] Mal.1:2

[336] Matt.24:12

[337] Rom.12:1 RV

[338] Eph.3:17-19

[339] Mal.1:6

[340] Ex.34:14

[341] Mal.3:13-14 cf.2 Cor.4:10-12

[342] Mal.1:6

[343] Jas.4:4

[344] Mal.1:7

[345] Mal.1:10

[346] C.T. Studd (1860-1931)

[347] See 2 Cor.5:10

[348] Mal.2:10

[349] Mk.12:30-31

[350] Mal.3:5

[351] Mal.2:14

[352] Mal.2:13

[353] Mal.2:16

[354] Mal.2:11

[355] See especially Ezra chapters 9 and 10

[356] 2 Cor.6:14

[357] Mal.2:17

[358] Mal.2:17-18; 3:14-15

[359] Mal.3:7

[360] Ibid.

[361] Mal.3:10

Did you love *The Message of the Minor Prophets*? Then you should read *Profiles of the Prophets* by Hayes Press!

This book provides a concise and informative overview of twelve of the most prominent prophets of the Bible - their call, mission and their methods: Elijah, Elisha, Isaiah, Jeremiah, Ezekiel, Daniel, Hosea, Amos, Jonah, Moses, Samuel and John the Baptist.

The final three chapters taking a look at the role and message of three lesser known prophets of the Old Testament.

Also by Hayes Press

Bible Studies
Bible Studies 1990 - First Samuel
Bible Studies 1991 - The First Letter of Paul to the Corinthians
Bible Studies 1993 - Second Samuel
Bible Studies 1994 - The Establishment and Development of
Churches of God
Bible Studies 1995 - The Kings of Judah and Israel from Solomon to
Asa
Bible Studies 1992 - The Second Letter of Paul to the Corinthians

Needed Truth
Needed Truth 1888
Needed Truth 2001
Needed Truth 2002
Needed Truth 2003
Needed Truth 2004
Needed Truth 2005
Needed Truth 2006
Needed Truth 2007
Needed Truth 2008
Needed Truth 2009
Needed Truth 2010

Needed Truth 2011
Needed Truth 2012
Needed Truth 2015
Needed Truth 1888-1988: A Centenary Review of Major Themes

Standalone
The Road Through Calvary: 40 Devotional Readings
Lovers of God's House
Different Discipleship: Jesus' Sermon on the Mount
The House of God: Past, Present and Future
The Kingdom of God
Knowing God: His Names and Nature
Churches of God: Their Biblical Constitution and Functions
Four Books About Jesus
Collected Writings On ... Exploring Biblical Fellowship
Collected Writings On ... Exploring Biblical Hope
Collected Writings On ... The Cross of Christ
Builders for God
Collected Writings On ... Exploring Biblical Faithfulness
Collected Writings On ... Exploring Biblical Joy
Possessing the Land: Spiritual Lessons from Joshua
Collected Writings On ... Exploring Biblical Holiness
Collected Writings On ... Exploring Biblical Faith
Collected Writings On ... Exploring Biblical Love
These Three Remain...Exploring Biblical Faith, Hope and Love
The Teaching and Testimony of the Apostles
Pressure Points - Biblical Advice for 20 of Life's Biggest Challenges
More Than a Saviour: Exploring the Person and Work of Jesus
The Psalms: Volumes 1-4 Boxset
The Faith: Outlines of Scripture Doctrine
Key Doctrines of the Christian Gospel

Is There a Purpose to Life?
Bible Covenants 101
The Hidden Christ - Volume 2: Types and Shadows in Offerings and Sacrifices
The Hidden Christ Volume 1: Types and Shadows in the Old Testament
The Hidden Christ - Volume 3: Types and Shadows in Genesis
Heavenly Meanings - The Parables of Jesus
Fisherman to Follower: The Life and Teaching of Simon Peter
Called to Serve: Lessons from the Levites
Needed Truth 2017 Issue 1
The Breaking of the Bread: Its History, Its Observance, Its Meaning
Spiritual Revivals of the Bible
An Introduction to the Book of Hebrews
The Holy Spirit and the Believer
The Psalms: Volume 1 - Thoughts on Key Themes
The Psalms: Volume 2 - Exploring Key Elements
The Psalms: Volume 3 - Surveying Key Sections
The Psalms: Volume 4 - Savouring Choice Selections
Profiles of the Prophets
The Hidden Christ - Volumes 1-4 Box Set
The Hidden Christ - Volume 4: Types and Shadows in Israel's Tabernacle
Baptism - Its Meaning and Teaching
Conflict and Controversy in the Church of God in Corinth
In the Shadow of Calvary: A Bible Study of John 12-17
Moses: God's Deliverer
Sparkling Facets: Bible Names and Titles of Jesus
A Little Book About Being Christlike
Keys to Church Growth
From Shepherd Boy to Sovereign: The Life of David
Back to Basics: A Guide to Essential Bible Teaching
An Introduction to the Holy Spirit

Israel and the Church in Bible Prophecy
"Growth and Fruit" and Other Writings by John Drain
15 Hot Topics For Today's Christian
Needed Truth Volume 2 1889
Studies on the Return of Christ
Studies on the Resurrection of Christ
Needed Truth Volume 3 1890
The Nations of the Old Testament: Their Relationship with Israel and
Bible Prophecy
The Message of the Minor Prophets
Insights from Isaiah
The Bible - Its Inspiration and Authority
Lessons from Ezra and Nehemiah
A Bible Study of God's Names For His People
Moses in One Hour

About the Publisher

Hayes Press (www.hayespress.org) is a registered charity in the United Kingdom, whose primary mission is to disseminate the Word of God, mainly through literature. It is one of the largest distributors of gospel tracts and leaflets in the United Kingdom, with over 100 titles and hundreds of thousands despatched annually. In addition to paperbacks and eBooks, Hayes Press also publishes Plus Eagles Wings, a fun and educational Bible magazine for children, and Golden Bells, a popular daily Bible reading calendar in wall or desk formats. Also available are over 100 Bibles in many different versions, shapes and sizes, Bible text posters and much more!

Lightning Source UK Ltd.
Milton Keynes UK
UKHW012007091121
393684UK00001B/126